Delivering Processing Instruction

Thanks to Grace Benati who contributed to the
development of the front cover of this book

Delivering Processing Instruction in Classrooms and in Virtual Contexts

Research and Practice

James F. Lee and Alessandro G. Benati

equinox

LONDON   OAKVILLE

Published by
UK: Equinox Publishing Ltd., Unit 6, The Village, 101 Amies St.,
London SW11 2JW
USA: DBBC, 28 Main Street, Oakville, CT 06779
www.equinoxpub.com

First published 2007

British Library Cataloguing-in-Publication Data
A catalogue record for this book is available from the British Library.

ISBN-13   978 1 84553 247 5   (hardback)
            978 1 84553 248 2   (paperback)

Library of Congress Cataloging-in-Publication Data
Delivering processing instruction in classrooms and in virtual
contexts : research and practice / Alessandro G. Benati and James F.
Lee.
      p. cm.
  Includes bibliographical references and index.
  ISBN-13: 978-1-84553-247-5 (hardback)
  ISBN-10: 1-84553-247-3 (hardback)
  ISBN-13: 978-1-84553-248-2 (pbk.)
  ISBN-10: 1-84553-248-1 (pbk.)
  1. Language and languages--Study and teaching--Psychological aspects.
  2. Second language acquisition. I. Lee, James F. II. Title.
  P53.7.B46 2007
  418.001'9--dc22
                              2006025257

Typeset by Catchline, Milton Keynes (www.catchline.com)
Printed and bound in Great Britain and the USA

Contents

Preface

From Alesandro Benati

The first time I encountered the topic of language acquisition was when I came to England in the late 1980s. I was employed as a language teacher in Adult Education. This stimulated my interest in various aspects of language teaching and learning. During this period I came across Bill VanPatten's input processing model and I became involved in research on the effects of processing instruction in the acquisition of the Italian language. I had always been interested in finding an alternative way of providing grammar instruction in the classroom and processing instruction seemed to provide an excellent way to incorporate grammar instruction in a communicative framework of language teaching. In the last ten years I have been involved in classroom-based research on the effects of processing instruction in the acquisition of Italian but also English and more recently Japanese. I must express my gratitude to Bill who has always supported me in my work and has provided me with priceless suggestions for improving my work in this area throughout the years. I was very honoured to be asked to participate to the Colloquium that Bill organised at the AAAL Conference in Salt Lake City in 2002 and where I met Andrew Farley and Wynne Wong who are excellent academics and colleagues.

I would like to thank James Lee and Bill VanPatten for writing the excellent book *Making Communicative Language Teaching Happens*. This book is the best I have ever read in the area of language teaching as theory and research are made accessible to everyone. This is a great gift.

I must express my gratitude to James Lee for his support and his valuable feedback in the various drafts of my chapters in this book. I met James at the Annual Conference of ALAA in 2005 in Melbourne where we presented some of the findings of processing instruction research that are included in this book. We spent most of our time eating in Italian restaurants and discussing issues related to research on processing instruction. Without his ideas and insights this book would not exist.

A special thanks to Paula Romero Lopez and Lucille Chapiro for taking part with me in the development of the materials for the PI and MOI in the case of the French, Italian and Spanish subjunctive of doubt project. Thanks are also due to Will Honeywill who developed the technical part of the activities. (www.wilburontheweb.co.uk/langproject). For this project we owe a special thanks to the University of Greenwich which financed the project.

I would also like to express my appreciation to the British Academy for its financial support in financing my travel to the Colloquium on Processing Instruction organised in Australia in September 2005. I would also like to thank all the students who participated to the classroom experiments presented in this book.

I must also express my gratitude to several people at the University of Greenwich who always supported and encouraged my work. Among them Jane Longmore and John Dunne.

Finally, I would like to thank my wife, Bernadette and my children, Francesco and Grace for moral support and for putting up with me and processing instruction.

From James F. Lee

I was part of the environment where Bill (VanPatten) formulated his ideas about input processing. I am very proud of the fact that I was a member of the dissertation committees of Teresa Cadierno, Cristina Sanz, and An Chung Cheng, a who's who of important contributors to Processing Instruction. In the Spring semester of 2005 I taught a graduate seminar on Input Processing at Indiana University. A significant component of the course was on Processing Instruction and so, I held up my former students (Teresa, Cristina, An Chung) as models for my current students. Among that group of 'current' students was Jorge Aguilar-Sánchez and Erin M. McNulty. They had approached me the previous year with a project on technology-enhanced instruction. Jorge wanted to create an online version of the entire textbook and test this online version (item by item) against the printed textbook. Given that we examined only two grammatical items, you might be able to imagine the conversations and discussions that got us there. Jorge sees the forest. Erin has great instincts and ideas, and, somehow always asks the right question to get me thinking. Erin's enthusiasm for Processing Instruction is infectious. I have enjoyed working with Jorge and Erin and fondly recall the first presentation we did of the research we are presenting in this volume.

Alessandro Benati's research on Processing Instruction is very important work. As he indicated above, we met in Melbourne, conceived of this book, and moved forward with it. Amazingly, he completes the work within the timeframe that he says he will and motivates me to work accordingly. I have greatly enjoyed working with Alessandro on this project.

Introduction

In this book we present the results of our most recent research in Processing Instruction, which is an approach to grammar instruction for second language learning. It derives its name from the fact that the instruction (both the explicit explanation as well as the practices) attempts to influence, alter, and/or improve the way learners process input. Processing Instruction contrasts with traditional grammar instruction in many ways, most principally in its focus on input whereas traditional grammar instruction focuses on learners' output. The greatest contribution of Processing Instruction to both theory and practice is the concept of 'structured input', a form of comprehensible input that has been manipulated in order to maximise learners' benefit of exposure to input. A growing body of research on the effects of Processing Instruction has given this approach to grammar instruction significant support. The positive effects of Processing Instruction have been found for a variety of languages (Spanish, French, Italian and English) and on a variety of morphological, syntactic and semantic linguistic items (past and future tense morphology, object pronouns, and subjunctive mood). Previous research has focused on two important issues. A body of research has compared the effects of Processing Instruction to those of other types of instruction. This work affirms the superiority of Processing Instruction over other types of instruction. Another body of research has examined the roles of explicit explanation and structured input practices in order to determine the source(s) of the effects of Processing Instruction on language development. This work affirms the importance of structured input activities.

This book focuses on a new issue for Processing Instruction, the role of technology in language learning. The principal aim of the book is to present the results of new unpublished empirical work that investigates the effects of delivering Processing Instruction in different modes. To accomplish this aim we will:

1. explain Processing Instruction, both its main theoretical underpinnings as well as the guidelines for developing structured input practices so that readers can critically evaluate this approach to grammar instruction;

2. review the empirical research conducted, to date, on Processing Instruction so that readers appreciate the foundation from which we work;

1

3. present the results of recent research on the effects of Processing Instruction and structured input activities;

4. draw appropriate conclusions about the role of technology in delivering PI.

We have chosen to organise this book around six main chapters.

*   In Chapter 1 we begin with a synopsis of VanPatten's theory of input processing, the one that most directly and greatly informs the practices of Processing Instruction (VanPatten 1996, 2003, 2004b). We then offer an explanation of the practice of Processing Instruction by defining and illustrating 'structured input', the concept most crucial to understanding Processing Instruction. The theme we will underscore is that Processing Instruction focuses learners on using forms in the input to gain access to meaning. Structured input exercises provide learners with practice in interpretation thus linking a form and its meaning. More specifically, when completing structured input practices, learners never produce the form being taught. Finally, we present and exemplify Lee and VanPatten's (1995, 2003) six guidelines for creating structured input activities.

*   In Chapter 2 we will provide a 'state-of-the-art' type review of all Processing Instruction research carried out so far. We begin this chapter by identifying and explicating the types of processing problems addressed in Processing Instruction research. Doing so allows us not only to highlight the linguistic items that have been investigated but provide a panoramic perspective on what morphological, syntactic, and semantic processing problems Processing Instruction has helped learners resolve. After this introduction to processing problems, we will then review work conducted under the two principle research foci for Processing Instruction. These foci are, understandably, the direction that the research base took. In order to promote Processing Instruction as a viable approach to grammar instruction, its proponents needed to prove its efficacy. The foci are:

    1. to compare the effects of Processing Instruction with those of other types of instructional treatments; and,

    2. to specify the role of structured input activities versus that of explicit information/explanation in the effects of Processing Instruction.

- In Chapter 3 we present the results of a classroom experiment investigating the possible effects of two different instructional interventions (structured input practice vs. traditional instruction) in the acquisition of Japanese past tense and use of affirmative vs. negative present tense forms. The relative effects of structured-input activities are compared to traditional output-based instruction on two principles (The Lexical Preference Principle and the Sentence Location Principle) used by L2 learners when processing input.

- In Chapter 4 we present the results of an empirical investigation on Processing Instruction in Spanish as a second language. In our first study, we manipulated three variables: mode of delivery, linguistic item, and time. We compared computer with classroom delivery of the materials. The two linguistic items investigated were Spanish preterite/imperfect distinction and affirmative informal commands. Additionally, we analysed the data for individual differences among learners for the effects of PI.

- In Chapter 5 we present the results of two distinct, but related, experiments that focus equally on two issues in Processing Instruction. First, the issue most central to the present book is that of modes of delivering instruction. To that end, we have created materials for use in a classroom (instructor + students + interaction) as well as having transposed these materials to a computer environment (terminal + individual student). Second, we extend the information we have on the issue of the effects of PI versus those of other types of instruction. Specifically, we compare PI to Meaning-based Output Instruction (MOI) on the acquisition of Italian and French subjunctive of doubt.

- Chapter 6 is the concluding chapter and it is divided in two parts, In part one we return the issues we presented in Chapter 2 when we reviewed the previous work on Processing Instruction. The two umbrella issues for Processing Instruction have been the effects of Processing Instruction versus those of other instruction types and the relative effects of Explanation versus Structured Input practices on learner performance. We will add our findings to the research base. In the second part we return to the issues we presented in Chapter 1 when we presented the theoretical foundations for PI and described and explained the nature of structured input. Based on our research we now draw appropriate pedagogical implications. We address modes of delivering instruction as well as address the insufficiency of input alone in grammar instruction and second language development. To that end, we will recommend an instructional sequence which begins with explanation and structured input practices but then moves to structured output practices (e.g., MOI) and interactive, task-based communicative activities.

1 The theory and practice of Processing Instruction

Part 1: Theory

Introduction

Cadierno (1995:180) pointed out that research in second language acquisition (SLA) has mainly been concerned with whether or not instruction has an effect on different aspects of language acquisition neglecting the fundamental questions of why and how instruction would make a difference in SLA. One avenue for researching the causes of the effects of instruction on SLA is, therefore, to examine the interaction between the way learners process input and the instruction to which they are exposed.

Terrell (1991) hypothesised a possible interaction between grammar instruction and the acquisition process itself in his binding\access model. Terrell (1991:53) defined explicit grammar instruction as 'the use of instructional strategies to draw the student's attention to or focus on form and/ or structure'. He posited (Terrell,1991:56) two main questions:

1. 'What psycholinguistic processes are utilised in input processing?'

2. 'How is the resulting information organised and accessed by the learner?'

He acknowledged that the primary source of acquisition is the input and he defined acquisition as 'the ability to comprehend and to produce meaningful utterances in the target language' (Terrell 1986:220). He characterised learners' comprehension of utterances in the input via two components:

1. The use of strategies to make sense of unknown forms in the input; and,

2. The association of meaning with new forms.

Terrell defined this latter component with the term 'binding', the cognitive process of linking a meaning to a new form in the target language. This process might be complex, particularly in the case of, for example, acquiring the grammatical gender markings of Italian adjectives, as in *bello\ bella* (beautiful\ masculine or beautiful\feminine). Learners must bind both words to the concept 'beautiful' and in addition the word *bello* must be linked to the grammatical concept 'masculine' and the word *bella* to 'feminine'. L2 learners must also access these words so that *bello* is used to describe masculine nouns and *bella* to describe feminine nouns. L2 learners must posit a semantic connection between the two words as well as a grammatical category of gender between *bello* and *bella* and between each of these two adjectives with other masculine or feminine adjectives.

Terrell (1991:60) suggested three ways in which explicit grammar instruction might indirectly support and affect the normal acquisition process. Two of the three functions of grammar instruction as it might affect acquisitional processes are relevant to input processing. First, grammar instruction can function as an advance organiser by providing learners with information about some forms and structures of a target language that will help them to process input. Terrell (1991:51) offered an example of advance organisers for college-level learners which refers to the Italian person-number verb morphemes; Italian adds endings to its verbs to indicate who is doing the action. For example the verb *parlo* ends in -o and means *I speak* while *parliamo* ends in *-iamo* and means *we speak*. At first, learners should concentrate on listening for the verb stem to understand what someone is saying. Later, learners will realise how these endings are quite helpful in understanding exactly who is doing what. Lee (2002a, 2002b) directed L2 learners to indicate each time they read a word that ended with *–á* and to try to figure out what the word meant. By doing so, learners could recognise the form and connect it to Spanish future tense meaning.

A second function for the role of grammar instruction in second language acquisition is as a meaning-form focuser for complex morphology. Grammar instruction can help the learner to establish a meaning-form relationship for morphologically complex forms. By a morphologically complex form, Terrell means non-salient or non- essential forms for understanding the meaning of an utterance, as is the case of many inflections. Inflections marking grammatical meanings such as tense are semantically redundant when they are accompanied by lexical temporal adverbs which also provide a temporal reference. Due to the high perceptual saliency of these lexical temporal adverbs, learners tend to pay more attention to the adverb marker of a given sentence and ignore the grammatical tense verb morphemes. For example, if the learner knows the Italian word for *domani*, then in the utterance *domani incontrerò Paolo al bar* (tomorrow, I will meet Paolo at the bar) the future tense is a redundant future marker. Furthermore, since *domani* has marked the sentence as future, the future markers on subsequent verbs are also redundant.

Terrell provides some suggestions on how instruction might help to make a redundant and non-salient grammatical meaning-form relationship salient in learner's input. Terrell underlines two requisites: first of all we should provide meaningful input and secondly the input should contain many instances of the same grammatical meaning-form relationship. (See Wong (2005) for more examples of flooding the input with forms.) Terrell (1991:60) then posed the question, 'does this concentration of many examples of a single meaning-form relationship in one activity result in the students being able to focus on meaning and form at the same time?'

A number of scholars has pointed out that L2 learners must attend to linguistic features in the input as well as to messages, form as well as meaning (VanPatten & Cadierno 1993, Hulstijn, 1989). VanPatten (1990) has, however, provided evidence to suggest that early-stage learners do not find it particularly easy to attend to both meaning and form in the input. Attending to both meaning and form places excessive demands on learners' attentional resources. Terrell (1991) suggested a remedy to help learners attend to meaning and grammatical markers at the same time. He claimed that only when learners were already familiar with the major lexical items in the input would they be able to process the grammatical markers. He argued that in a grammatically focused input activity the lexical load should be light so that students do not have to expend much processing time in general form-meaning access. Terrell (1991:60) concluded that instruction with low lexical load coupled with a flood of a single meaning-form relationship would help learners to attend to and process non-salient, redundant grammatical forms.

VanPatten (1996:17) has suggested that a central issue for SLA is 'how learners' internal processors allocate attentional resources during on-line processing'. The question is, then, what causes certain stimuli in the input to be detected and not others? Because L2 learners' attentional capacity is limited, and exhausts itself quickly, only certain features will receive attention at any given time during the processing of a sentence. Which ones?

Input Processing

Because VanPatten has always recognised the essential role of input in SLA, he devised form-focused instruction directed at how learners process input, and he termed this instruction Processing Instruction (PI) (1996, 2002, 2004a,

2004b). PI is derived from and consistent with VanPatten's model of input processing, which refers to three sets of acquisitional processes, as depicted below (adapted from VanPatten, 1996:41).

process 1   process 2   process 3

INPUT → INTAKE → DEVELOPING SYSTEM → OUTPUT

Figure 1.1: VanPatten's schematic of second language acquisition

These processes take linguistic data in the input, convert it to intake, and make the intake available to the developing system. VanPatten's model of input processing, and his approach to grammar instruction, centers on the first and initial set of processes through which learners interact with input, those are the processes through which learners attend to form and meaning and connect forms in the input with their meanings (VanPatten 2004b: 5).

As discussed by VanPatten (1996:8) what learners do with and to input during comprehension, which is how intake is derived, is called input processing (process 1). Intake is the small amount of linguistic data that learners have perceived and processed in the input. Initially, only a portion of the input is processed due to processing limitations and heuristics. Because learners filter input, not all input becomes intake. The second set of processes (2) refers to all those processes that allow the intake (the form-meaning connections that were made) to become part of the acquired or developing system. Processes involved in the incorporation of intake into the developing system are called 'accommodation' and 'restructuring'. The third set of processes (3) consists of those processes by which learners access their developing systems in order to produce the L2.

We are interested primarily on the first set of processes, those by which input becomes intake. Only part of the input is passed as intake into the developing system and eventually available for learners to access for output production. The recognition of the essential role of learners in processing input and creating intake has raised a number of questions on the nature of input processing. One important question for instructed second language acquisition is: Can input processing be manipulated, altered or enhanced in order to make intake better in both quantity and quality? Sharwood-Smith (1993) provided some general ideas about enhanced input whereas VanPatten (1993) provided very principled ones.

Input processing is concerned with those psycholinguistic mechanisms and cognitive strategies by which learners derive intake from input. It is the forms in the input to which learners have connected meanings and, more specifically, the form-meaning connections that they have held on to. Changing the way learners process input should affect the quality and/or quality of intake and, should, consequently, affect the developing system.

The question is how do learners initially perceive and process linguistic data in the language they hear or read. In VanPatten's model, working memory plays a pivotal role and the processing principles at the basis of the model are formulated taking into consideration human limited capacity for processing. (See Harrington 2004 for further discussion of VanPatten's model vis a vis processing capacity limitations.)

The two main sub-processes in input processing are: making form-meaning connections and parsing. Learners make form-meaning connections from the input they receive as they connect particular meanings to particular forms (grammatical or lexical). Parsing consists of the process of mapping syntactic structure in the sentence so that the learner can ascertain what is the subject and what is the object in a sentence. Research on input processing attempts to describe: what linguistic data learners attend to during comprehension, which ones they do not attend to, what grammatical roles learners assign to nouns and how position in an utterance influences what gets processed. (See Harrington 2004 for further discussion of VanPatten's model vis a vis parsing).

VanPatten has developed his model a great deal since 1996, in response both to empirical research on PI and to the model's critics. In 1996 he reviewed research on first and second language processing with an eye to identifying which features of the input learners attend to, which they ignore, and whether learners' direct their attention in a principled way. His analysis yielded a model captured by three principles and their corollaries.

P1.   Learners process input for meaning before the process it for form.

P1(a). Learners process content words in the input before anything else.

P1(b). Learners prefer processing lexical items to grammatical items (e.g., morphological markings) for semantic information.

P1(c). Learners prefer processing 'more meaningful' morphology before 'less' or 'nonmeaningful' morphology.

P2.   For learners to process form that is not meaningful, they must be able to process informational or communicative content at no (or little) cost to attention. (VanPatten 1996: 14–15)

P3.   Learners possess a default strategy that assigns the role of agent to the first noun (phrase) they encounter in a sentence. We call this the 'first noun strategy.'

P3(a). The first noun strategy can be overridden by lexical semantics and event probabilities.

P3(b). Learners will adopt other processing strategies for grammatical role assignment only after their developing system has incorporated other cues (e.g., case markings, acoustic stress). (VanPatten 1996:32)

By 2004, VanPatten had reworked the model significantly to such end that it now consists of two main principles, each with several subprinciples. (His discussion in 2004b traces the development of the model to its present form. We direct the reader who is interested in these details to his discussion.) The two main principles are:

Principle 1. The Primacy of Meaning Principle. Learners process input for meaning before they process for form. (VanPatten 2004b: 7)

Principle 2. The First Noun Principle. Learners tend to process the first noun or pronoun they encounter in a sentence as the subject or agent. (VanPatten 2004b: 15)

We present below the corollaries for Principle 1 (VanPatten (2004b: 14). Each now carries its own name, which allows for better clarity of reference. These corollaries are phrased in ways that show how flexible learners' verbal behaviour can be.

P 1a.   The Primacy of Content Words Principle: learners process content words in the input before anything else.

P 1b.   The Lexical Preference Principle: learners will tend to rely on lexical items as opposed to grammatical form to get meaning when both encode the same semantic information.

P 1c.   The Preference for Nonredundancy Principle: learners are more likely to process nonredundant meaningful grammatical form before they process redundant meaningful forms.

P 1d. The Meaning-Before-Non Meaning Principle: learners are more likely to process meaningful grammatical forms before nonmeaningful forms irrespective of redundancy.

P 1e. The Availability of Resources Principle: for learners to process either redundant meaningful grammatical forms or nonmeaningful forms, the processing of overall sentential meaning must not drain available processing resources.

P 1f. The Sentence Location Principle: learners tend to process items in sentence initial position before those in final position and those in medial position.

We now present the corollaries to Principle 2 (VanPatten 2004b: 18). These corollaries can be seen as constraints on the operation of the First Noun Principle.

P 2a. The Lexical Semantics Principle: learners may rely on lexical semantics, where possible, instead of word order to interpret sentences.

P 2b. The Event Probabilities Principle: learners may rely on event probabilities, where possible, instead of word order to interpret sentences.

P 2c. The Contextual Constraint Principle: learners may rely less on the First Noun Principle if preceding context constraints the possible interpretation of a clause or sentence.

Principle 1 and its corollaries are most directly relevant to the research we present in the next section of the book. We will use examples of the linguistic items we investigated in order to exemplify the principles.

The first principle (P1) which states that learners are driven to look for the message in the input before they look at how that message is grammatically encoded, is consistent with the observations by other researchers, in particular Sharwood-Smith (1993) who argues that adult second language learners' attention is directed towards meaning when they are processing input. The question addressed by VanPatten (1996:18) is: when learners aim to extract meaning from the input, 'which aspects of the input will aid them'? As demonstrated both by Sharwood-Smith (1986) and VanPatten (1990), learners will be directed toward the detection of content words in order to grasp the meaning of an utterance. Early stage learners will use words as building blocks of meaning as they often do not have sufficient attentional resources to process form. The first corollary (P1.a), the primacy of content words, is supported by first and second language research. Evidence in L2 research comes from both an introspection study (Mangubhai 1991) and experimental studies (Hulstijn 1989, VanPatten 1990, Bransdorfer 1989). In particular VanPatten (1990) has shown that learners can be directed to attend to the key lexical items without loss of propositional content when processing input but cannot be directed to attend to grammatical markers without loss of propositional content.

In the second corollary (P1.b), the lexical preference principle, VanPatten asserts that learners prefer processing lexical items to grammatical items (e.g., morphology) for semantic information. This principle is a direct consequence of VanPatten's first principle. A great number of grammatical features encodes some kind of semantic information. In the case of verbal inflection the Italian verbal inflection -*ato* encodes past as in *parlato*. The same semantic notion is, however, also expressed in Italian by words such as *ieri* (yesterday) or *l'anno passato* (last year). Given, as postulated in the first corollary (Principle 1a), that learners are driven to process content words before anything else, they would attend to lexical temporal references of 'pastness' before verbal inflections of the past tense. Our research with Japanese provides another example. In the Japanese sentence *Kinou watashi wa Peter to gekijyou ni ikimashita* (Yesterday I went to the theatre with Peter) learners would find it easier to tag the lexical temporal adverb Kinou (yesterday) for pastness than they would to identify and process the past tense form *ikimashita*. If learners do not process the grammatical forms, then they do not derive intake that has incorporated them. The developing system stagnates if it does not receive intake or form-meaning connections.

Lexical preference is well documented by both empirical studies on processing (Musumeci 1989, Cadierno & Glass 1990, Lee, Cadierno, Glass &VanPatten 1997, Lee 1999) and research into the acquisition of tense, i.e., learners' output (Bardovi-Harlig 1992, Klein 1986). The studies on the acquisition of tense have focused on how tense is first encoded in learners' output. This research has provided evidence that learners typically mark time early in the acquisition of verb morphology through lexical items (*oggi, domani...*) and only subsequently add verb tense markings. Learners prefer to mark tense lexically before they mark it morphologically.

From the processing side, we offer Musumeci (1989) as an example. She conducted a cross-linguistic study (Italian, French, and Spanish) in which she examined L2 learners' tense assignment for sentences they heard under different conditions. Among the conditions was the presence or absence of lexical temporal markers in the input. Overall, the results confirmed that the main factor determining correct tense assignment was the presence or absence of lexical temporal adverbs in the input sentences. The inclusion of lexical items in the input significantly improved learners' correct tense assignment (Musumeci 1989:127). Musumeci's study revealed that early stage learners use, if not rely on, lexical items in order to assign tense.

VanPatten's third corollary (P1.c) is currently formulated as the meaningful-before-nonmeaningful principle. Its roots lie in the construct of a grammatical item's communicative value to the learner. VanPatten (1996:24) stated that 'it is the relative communicative value of a grammatical form that plays a major role in determining the learner's attention to it during input processing and the likelihood of its becoming detected and thus part of intake'. Communicative value refers to the relative contribution a grammatical item makes to the meaning of an utterance from a second language learner's perspective. In order to establish whether a linguistic form has low or high communicative value, we need to follow two criteria: 1. inherent referential meaning, and, 2. semantic redundancy. Word-final inflections on adjectives (*o* & *a*) in Italian are, for example, low in communicative value because they are redundant and lack inherent semantic value. In the Italian phrase *la penna rossa* (the red pen), *rossa* ends in -*a*- because the noun it modifies is grammatically feminine. The -*a* does not carry any inherent referential meaning in this phrase. In addition, -*a* characterises how three words in the noun phrase end; the grammatical marker is, therefore, highly redundant. If learners do not need the element to process the meaning of the phrase, then they most likely will not process it.

The sixth corollary (P1.f) lays out a hierarchy of difficulty, or rather a hierarchy of processing saliency, with regard to L2 features. In a sentence like *Penso che Paolo sia un buon giocatore* (I think that Paul is a good player) the easiest forms to process are those located in salient positions, specifically, initial position (*Penso*) within an utterance. The second easiest forms to process occur in the other salient position, utterance-final position (*un buon giocatore*). Finally, the most difficult forms to process are those that occur in utterance-medial position (*sia*). We tend to pay attention to what comes first (primacy) and what comes last (recency). Initial and final positions are privileged in terms of processing. The problem for second language learners is that many grammatical features occur in sentence medial position. In the French utterance *Je ne pense pas que Gérard Depardieu soit très elegant* (I do not think that Gérard Depardieu is very elegant) the subjunctive form is located in medial position and therefore the most difficult form to process in the sentence. Learners do not attend to sentence medial position. The consequence for second language acquisition is that no intake is derived around the form.

Part 2: Practice

Processing Instruction

One of the main implications drawn from the previous paragraphs for instruction in an input processing framework is that it should take into account the psycholinguistic processes utilised in input processing (strategies and mechanisms used by L2 learners to process input). The main role for form-focused instruction then becomes to manipulate, enhance and alter input processing in order to make intake grammatically richer. This pedagogy must take as its point of departure how grammatical forms are processed. This pedagogy must work with input and with the processes learners use to take in linguistic data from that input. Now that we have VanPatten's model of input processing, we have some idea of what learners are doing with input when they are asked to comprehend it and we have a framework for discussing what learners do with input. We can now explore VanPatten's approach to grammar instruction, i.e., PI. Once we know what learners do with input, we can devise an input-based pedagogy, one that seeks to help learners derive richer intake from the input (VanPatten 1996: 55; Wong 2004a: 33).

As part of the rationale for PI, VanPatten pointed out that 'traditional' grammar instruction relied on output practices. He defines traditional instruction (TI) as 'explanation plus output practices that moves learners from mechanical to communicative drills' (VanPatten 2000: 54). Unlike TI the purpose of PI is to change the way learners attend to and process input considering that acquisition is an input-dependent process and takes place when learners are exposed to comprehensible meaning-bearing input (Lee & VanPatten 2003). TI consisting of drills in which learner output is manipulated and the instruction is divorced from meaning or communication is not an effective method for enhancing language acquisition (Wong & VanPatten 2003).

Despite the fact that language classrooms are becoming more and more communicative, the way grammar is presented and practised is still very traditional. It consists of grammatical explanations (paradigmatic presentation) followed by output practice (grammar rules and paradigms). The output-led path is still of central importance in foreign language courses at Universities, despite the fact that one can assume that pedagogical principles and practices should reflect theory and research in SLA. In most of the traditional approaches to grammar instruction L2 learners are given an explicit explanation of the rules of a form/structure of a target language, and then they practice these rules through various output exercises. Paulston (1972) has described a typical sequence of oral grammar practice in which mechanical practice precedes meaningful and communicative practices. This hierarchy reflects the way grammar is still taught and practiced in the foreign language classroom, despite language classroom becoming more and more communicative.

Unlike TI where instruction focuses on the manipulation of the learners' output to effect changes in their developing system, PI aims to change the way input is perceived and processed by language learners (see below).

INPUT → INTAKE → DEVELOPING SYSTEM → OUTPUT

↑

Output-based instruction   output-based practice

INPUT → INTAKE → DEVELOPING SYSTEM → OUTPUT

↑

input-based practice

Figure 1.2: Processing Instruction

As pointed out earlier, this approach to grammar instruction is consistent with an input processing perspective in SLA. As shown in Figure 1.2, input-based practice should logically precede output-based practice. Unlike output-based instruction which emphasised grammar rules and oral/written production practice, the purpose of processing instruction is to alter how learners process input and to encourage better form-meaning mappings which result in a grammatically richer intake. In the case of tense markers, processing instruction can make these redundant and non-salient grammatical meaning-form relationships more salient in the learner's input as well as teach learners how to perceive these forms in the input. Given the emphasis on learners' input rather than focusing on the output, the type of practice provided by the processing instruction approach consists of activities that offer the opportunity to interpret the meaning-form relationship correctly without any practice in producing the targeted form or structure.

As outlined by VanPatten (1996: 84) 'simply bringing a form to someone's attention is not a guarantee that it gets processed or processed correctly... For acquisition to happen the intake must continually provide the developing system with examples of correct form-meaning connections that are the result of input processing'. PI, contrary to 'negative enhancement', does not address the role of output errors since it is solely concerned with the processing of input data. PI might be considered, as mentioned earlier, as a type of 'consciousness-raising'; in the sense that, as indicated by VanPatten (1996: 85) it 'does not seek to pour knowledge of any kind into learners' heads; it assists certain processes that can aid the growth of the developing system over time'. However, the ultimate scope of processing instruction is not about raising learners' consciousness about a grammatical form but rather to enrich learners' intake.

PI is, as VanPatten (1996) claimed, 'a psycholinguistically motivated approach to focus on form' whose main aim is to teach grammar without sacrificing either communication or learning-centred activities. It includes grammatical explanation and grammatical practice, but a specific type of grammatical practice called structured input.

PI's main objective is to help learners circumvent ineffective processing strategies or to instill appropriate processing strategies so that they derive better intake from the input. It consists of three basic components:

a) explicit information about a linguistic form/structure;

b) information about a processing principle;

c) structured input activities.

We now offer examples of each component.

PI is grammar instruction and so it does provide learners explicit information about the form. Examples of Italian, Spanish and English follow.

ITALIAN

Explicit information

You have probably noticed descriptive adjectives have different gender:

In Italian adjectives must agree in number and gender to the noun they modify.

Masculine = o	Feminine = a
bello	bella
un ragazzo bello	una ragazza bella
Clinton è bello	Claudia Schiffer è bella

You must pay attention to the adjective ending in order to understand who and what we are referring to. In addition to that, you need to understand the meaning of the sentence containing the adjective.

SPANISH

Explicit Information

*Spanish simple past tense is called **pretérito indefinido**. This past tense has different forms from the present tense. The **pretérito indefinido** serves to report actions, events, and states that are viewed as having been completed in the past.*

Notice that: *Past form is usually accompanied by **temporal adverbs** that will indicate that the action has already happened in the past. Here are some of the most common ones: ayer (yesterday), la semana pasada (last week), anteayer (the day before yesterday), anoche (last night), etc. However, although these adverbs are a good clue to know that an action has occurred in the past, **they are not always present** in the sentences. That is why it is very important for you to recognise past tense forms. Third person singular. Let's see now **the third person singular** of the regular verbs in the past.*

El/ ella/ usted

se acostó	comió
cenó	salió
habló	vivió

***There are three clues that will help you to recognise the third person singular past verb forms: 1.** The past tense (third person) of regular **-AR verbs** is formed by adding the ending –ó to the root of the verb, which is obtained by deleting the –AR ending from the infinitive **2.** The past tense (third person) of regular **–ER, -IR verbs** is formed by adding the ending –ió to the root of the verb, which is obtained by deleting the –ER, or –IR endings from the infinitive. **Notice** that –er and-ir verbs share the same endings, which will be easier for you to remember them **3.** Most of the third person past tense verbs end in a **stressed or accented vowel**, which is very important to produce, both in oral and written modes. This is crucial in order to distinguish past from the present tense forms (which are unaccented)*

ENGLISH

Explicit Information

The past simple tense is one of the tenses most used to talk about events in the past. It does refer to finished actions and events. Very often the English Past Simple Tense end in –ed:

> *I invited John for lunch*
> *I played tennis with Paula*

When you talk about a finished time in the past, the English Past Simple Tense is often accompanied by a temporal adverb.

> *Yesterday I smoked 20 cigarettes*

DO NOT RELY ON THE TEMPORAL ADVERB TO UNDERSTAND WHEN THE ACTION TAKES PLACE AS SOMETIME YOU CAN HEAR A SENTENCE WITHOUT THE TEMPORAL ADVERB.

YOU MUST PAY ATTENTION THE TENSE ENDING TO UNDERSTAND WHEN THE ACTION TAKES PLACE.

IN THE CASE OF DESCRIBING PAST EVENTS PAY ATTENTION TO THE ENDING OF THE VERB: -ed

The 'P' in PI stands for processing and so PI includes explicit information about processing input. Learners are informed about a particular processing strategy that negatively affect their picking up of the form or structure such as the first noun strategy, or are informed about where to focus their processing effort. In the previous examples of explicit information, we highlighted the portion of the explanation that referred to processing problems and strategies.

Finally, the most critical part of PI is structured input (see the review of literature in Chapter 2). Learners who receive PI are pushed to process the form or structure for its meaning through structured input activities. In structured input activities the input is manipulated in particular ways to push learners to become dependent on form and structure to get meaning. As outlined by Wong (2004b) PI 'pushes learners to abandon their inefficient processing strategies for more optimal ones so that better form-meaning connections are made' (p.35). Given how crucial structured input activities are to PI, we now offer a description of them as well as several examples.

Structured input activities

VanPatten and Sanz (1995) and Lee and VanPatten (1995, 2003) have produced the following guidelines for structured input activities. (See also Farley 2005 and Wong 2005 for more suggestions on creating structured input activities.)

A) Present one thing at a time.

B) Keep meaning in focus.

C) Move from sentences to connected discourse.

D) Use both oral and written input.

E) Have learners do something with the input.

F) Keep learners' processing strategies in mind.

A) Paradigms and rules should be broken down into smaller parts and taught one at the time during the course of the lesson (samples in Italian, Spanish and English are provided in this chapter). Students are presented with the linguistic feature (see examples of explicit information in the previous paragraph) before being exposed to structured input activities. If learners receive information on only one form at a time, this will increase their chance to make correct form-meaning connections. Learners will then be provided with more opportunities to engage in meaningful practice and receive less grammar explanation.

B) Learners should be encouraged to make form-meaning connections through structured input activities (see Activities A-E). As pointed out by VanPatten (1996:68) 'if meaning is absent or if learners do not have to pay attention to meaning to complete the activity, then there is not enhancement of input processing'. In all the processing instruction activities presented in this chapter meaning is always kept in focus. Learners must be able to complete an activity by understanding what they hear or they see.

C) In SIA short sentences should be used initially as learners would struggle if the utterance is too long, A long sentence would overload their working memory and would make it difficult for learners to process a new form. Lee and VanPatten (2003) suggest that we should move gradually from a short sentence to a longer sentence and then to connected discourse before providing learners with output activities.

D) Activities which combine oral and written input should be used as some learners respond better to one than the other. This is in order to account for individual differences.

E) Learners must be engaged in processing the input sentences and must respond to the input sentence in some way through referential and affective types of structured input activities. Learners should always be engaged in doing something with the input they receive instead of just being passive recipients of input (see referential and affective activities).

F) Learners' attention should be guided not to rely on natural processing strategies. Activities in which the input is structured to alter learners reliance on one particular processing principle should be created. This is certainly the most important guideline for developing SIA as the main goal of this instructional technique is to help learners to move away from inefficient processing strategies so that they can adopt better ones.

Structured input activities (SIA) help L2 learners to process target forms that might otherwise not be processed or not be processed correctly. The first step in developing SIA is to identify the processing problem first. For example, learners of Japanese tend to pay more attention to content words such as the temporal adverb *Kinou*, than to the past form *ikimashita*, as both encode pastness. Once the processing problem has been identified we structure the input by removing the content word in the sentence so that learners will have to pay attention, notice and process those grammatical items that otherwise would be missed. During SIA learners are encouraged to make form-meaning connections. As VanPatten (1996:68) points out, 'if meaning is absent or if learners do not have to pay attention to meaning to complete the activity, then there is no enhancement of input processing'. Learners must be engaged in processing the input sentences and must respond to the input sentence in some way.

There are two types of SIA: referential and affective activities. Referential activities are those for which there is a right or wrong answer and for which the learner must rely on the targeted grammatical form to get meaning. The main purpose of these type of activities is to check whether learners are making the correct form-meaning connections. For example, in Activity A, learners must process the verbal inflection to temporal reference. The answer is correct or incorrect. In Activity B, learners listen for an expression of certainty or doubt and then select the correct ending to the sentence.

Activity A

Listen to the following sentences in Japanese and determine if we refer to today or last week.

        Senshu Kyo
1.   ☐   ☐
2.   ☐   ☐
3.   ☐   ☐
4.   ☐   ☐
5.   ☐   ☐

Sentence heard by learner:

1. *Totemo ii hon o yomimashita*
2. *Resutoran de hatarakimashita*
3. *Gekijyou ni ikimasu*
4. *Paul to kouen o arukimashita*
5. *Gengogaku o benkyou shimasu*

Activity B   « Personaggi Famosi »

You will hear the beginning part of a sentence that deals with facts and opinions about famous people. Based on what you hear, place a check mark by the phrase that best completes each statement.

1)
.... è un bugiardo
.... sia un bugiardo
2)
.... è un genio della regia
.... sia un genio della regia
3)
.... è una donna attraente
.... sia una donna attraente
4)
.... ha molti soldi
..........abbia molti soldi
5)
.... sa cantare
..........sappia cantare

Sentence heard by learner:

1. *È certo che George Bush...*
2. *Non penso che Tarantino....*
3. *Non credo che Jodie Foster...*
4. *È sicuro che la Regina...*
5. *Non penso che Celine Dion...*

Affective structured input activities are those in which learners are required to express an opinion, belief, or indicate some other affective response to real world information. In Activity C, they agree or disagree with statements made about politicians. In none of these activities, do learners produce the forms.

Activity C   (Il politico modello)

Read the statements below and indicate whether you agree or do not agree with each statement about a good politician.

Quali sono le caratteristiche di un politico modello? Non credo che ...

		Sono d'accordo	Non sono d'accordo
1	sia onesto	❏	❏
2	abbia relazioni extra coniugali	❏	❏
3	ascolti la gente	❏	❏
4	sia disonesto	❏	❏
5	faccia favori agli amici	❏	❏
6	dica la verità	❏	❏
7	abbia poco tempo per la famiglia	❏	❏
8	piaccia alla gente	❏	❏
9	rispetti la legge	❏	❏
10	beva molto	❏	❏

Of course, we can combine both referential and affective elements in a single activity. In Activity D learners must process the input, specifically the adjectival ending, to determine whether the statement they hear refers to Bill Clinton or Monica Lewinsky. Learners are obliged to attend to the grammatical markers (gender agreement in Italian) in order to establish to whom the sentence was referring. The answer is correct or incorrect. At the same time, learners must process each sentence for its meaning in order to agree or disagree with the statement.

Activity D

Listen to each sentence in which a person is described and determine which person is described. Then indicate whether you agree or disagree.

1.   □ Bill Clinton   □ Monica Lewinsky

     □ agree   □ disagree

2.   □ Bill Clinton   □ Monica Lewinsky

     □ agree   □ disagree

3.   □ Bill Clinton   □ Monica Lewinsky

   □ agree   □ disagree

Sentence heard by learner:

   1. *È bella*
   2. *È dinamico*
   3. *È carismatico*

In Activity E learners must process the subjunctive or indicative forms to determine whether or not doubt is expressed. Learners must also process each sentence for its meaning in order to complete the task of agreeing or disagreeing with the content of the sentences.

Activity E

You will here the second half of a sentence concerning your teacher. First, tick the appropriate opinion phrase to fit each statement, then say if you agree or not which each statement.

			D'accordo	**Non d'accordo**
	□	a. Non penso che …		
1	□	b. Sono certo che…	□	□
	□	a. Dubito che…		
2	□	b. So che…	□	□
	□	a. Sono sicuro che…		
3	□	b. Non Penso che…	□	□

Sentence heard by learner:

   1. *sia sposato*
   2. *ha una vespa*
   3. *sia ricco*

In Activities F and G we removed temporal adverbs from the sentences learners heard so that the verb endings would be the only indicators of tense. Learners must use verbal morphology as indicator of tense since the lexical indicators of tense were absent in order to establish when the action described takes place (present vs. future and present vs. past).

Activity F

You are going to hear some sentences in Italian. Select whether each sentence you hear occurred in the present or the future. **Keep in mind that future tense forms have the spoken stress in the vowel of the endings (3rd person)**

1. a) present   b) future

2. a) present   b) future

3. a) present   b) future

4. a) present   b) future

5. a) present   b) future

Sentence heard by learner:

1. *guardo il film in televisione*
2. *tornerai in treno con tuo fratello*
3. *resto a casa tutto il giorno*
4. *passerò le prossime vacanze con amici*
5. *pranzo a casa con i miei genitori*

Activity G

You will hear 10 sentences and you need to determine whether the action is taking place now (present) or has already taken place (past).

	Present	**Past**
1.	□	□
2.	□	□

Sentence heard by learner:

1. *I listen to music*
2. *I walked to the park*

Lee and VanPatten (1995:109) have proposed various types of SIA (binary options, matching, supplying information, selecting alternatives). In the case of the first example of binary option activity provided (Activity H) below learners must decide which of the two statements they agree or disagree with and then at the end establish whether they are pessimistic or optimistic people. In the case of the second binary option activity (Activity I) learners must establish whether the statements are true or false and then express their opinions about the habits of a typical student.

Activity H   Binary Options

Step 1

Indicate whether or not you agree or disagree with each of the predictions listed below. Some of them will probably happen in the next ten years.

	Agree	Disagree
1. Uno scenziato troverà la cura per l'AIDS		
2. Una donna diventerà presidente degli USA		
3. Si scoprirà la cura per il cancro		
4. L'Irlanda del Nord diventerà repubblica		

Step 2

Confirm your answers with your partner. Sei ' pessimista' o 'ottimista'.

Activity I   More Binary Options

Step 1

Read the following sentences and state whether they are true or not true for a typical student at the University

	Vero	Falso
Lavora a tempo pieno		
Studia tutto il giorno		
Va a letto presto		
Lavora part-time		
Mangia poco		

Guarda Eastenders
Consulta libri
Va a dormire tardi
Arriva all'Università in bici
Guadagna molti soldi

Step 2

Look at the statements you checked as true. Are you a typical student? As you did the activity did you notice the ending of the verb?

In the matching activity (Activity J) learners must determine which is the person described and then express their view about whether or not they agree or disagree with the statement they heard.

Activity J   Matching

Step 1

Listen to each sentence in which a person is described. First, determine which person is being described.

1.	Luciano Pavarotti	Sofia Lauren
	agree	disagree
2.	Luciano Pavarotti	Sofia Lauren
	agree	disagree
3.	Luciano Pavarotti	Sofia Lauren
	agree	disagree
4.	Luciano Pavarotti	Sofia Lauren
	agree	disagree

1. *È grasso*
2. *È brutta*
3. *È antipatico*
4. *È grassa*

Step 2

Now indicate whether you agree or disagree.

In the second matching activity (Activity K) learners must establish whether the action takes place in the present or the future and then match the time of the events with the words in the second list.

Activity K   More Matching

Listen to each sentences. First decide if the sentences are in the present or in the future. Then select the name of the person or country that answers the questions.

1.	present	Italia ———
	future	Irlanda ———
		Francia ———
2.	present	The Queen ———
	future	Tony Blair ———
		Sean Connery ———
3.	present	France ———
	future	Italy ———
		England ———
4.	present	Ravanelli ———
	future	Zola ———
		Baggio ———
5.	present	Il Papa ———
	future	Bill Clinton ———
		The Queen ———
6.	present	Germany ———
	future	Turkey ———
		France ———

Sentence heard by learner:

1. *diventerà un paese unito*
2. *abita a Buckingam Palace*
3. *ospiterà i campionati del mondo di calcio*
4. *lavora per il Chelsea*
5. *visiterà l'Irlanda del Nord*
6. *diventerà un membro della comunità europea*

In the case of the supplying information (see Activity L below) type of structured input activities learners are required to complete part of a sentence and then determine whether the same thing described applies to them. Note that in Step 2, learners speak. Their production includes the target form, but in this case, they are merely reading off a sentence provided in the input.

Activity L   Supplying Information

Step 1

Your teacher reads a short passage. Give as many details as possible by completing the following sentences. The student who gets more details wins.

   1.   Alessandro si sveglia _____
   2.   non si alza subito dato che_____
   3.   si prepara_____

Step 2

Look at the details you have collected and read a sentence to the class and say whether or not the same thing applies to you.

   Model: Alessandro si sveglia molto tardi la mattina, and so do I.
               Alessandro si sveglia molto tardi la mattina, but I do not.

In the selecting alternatives type activity (see Activity M) learners must select a phrase that best completes a statement provided.

Activity M   Selecting Alternatives

Step 1

Select the phrase that best completes each statement about your instructor.

   1 Appena arriva a casa il mio insegnante....
   a) fa una doccia   b) gioca con i bambini
   c) guarda la tele   d) fa qualcos'altro...

   2 Quando è l'ora della cena.....
   a) prepara da mangiare   b) ordina una pizza
   c) aiuta sua moglie a cucinare   d) aspetta la cena

Step 2

Now your instructor will tell you whether you are correct or not

Activity N offers learners alternatives from which to select logical responses. Learners hear a series of possible activities and must circle the logical ones.

Activity N   More Selecting Alternatives

You are going to hear several activities that some people will do. Circle the letter of the activities that are not logical and say why there are not.

1. In Europa i miei genitori ....
    a   b   c   d

2. Paolo e Francesca passeranno le vacanze di Natale e ....
    a   b   c   d

3. I miei amici visiteranno Londra e ....
    a   b   c   d

4. se è bel tempo Paolo e Giulia usciranno e ....
    a   b   c   d

Sentence heard by learner:

1. a)   *visiteranno il Museo del Louvre*
    b)   *pranzeranno in un buon ristorante francese*
    c)   *visiteranno le piramidi di Il Cairo*
    d)   *passeranno due giorni a Roma*

2. a)   *resteranno a casa con I loro parenti*
    b)   *lavoreranno*
    c)   *mangieranno molto*
    d)   *chiacchereranno*

3. a)   *visiteranno Harrowds*
    b)   *prenderanno una birra*
    c)   *prenderanno il sole al mare*
    d)   *incontreranno la Regina*

4. a)   *usciranno*
    b)   *resteranno in casa*
    c)   *incontreranno amici*
    d)   *prenderanno la bicicletta*

SIA can be produced to practice any grammatical form/structure for which there is a processing problem. The overall scope of structured input activities is to affect learners processing strategies so that learners will process input for both form and meaning in a more accurate way. SI is a very successful enhancement technique not only in making learners establish the correct form-meaning connections but also in providing communicative activities that encourage meaningful exchange of information.

2 Processing Instruction research: foci and findings

VanPatten first described publicly Processing Instruction (PI) in 1993 in his exposition of what grammar instruction could be in an acquisition-rich classroom (VanPatten, 1993). Over time, the description gained depth, breadth and precision as well as increased empirical foundation (Lee and VanPatten, 1995, 2003; VanPatten, 1996, 2003, 2004a). As an approach to grammar instruction, PI has generated numerous empirical investigations documenting its effects on second language development. In this chapter we will review the research conducted to date demonstrating a very consistent set of findings on the effects of PI and the elements of PI that cause those effects. In order to appreciate the breadth of the research base, we begin with an account of the linguistic items that have been investigated. Researchers have selected these items because they present second language learners with various processing problems. Quite simply, if the instruction does not address a processing problem, then it is not PI. Learners tend to approach these linguistic items with either inappropriate or incorrect processing strategies. The ultimate problem (versus the idea of ultimate attainment) when learners use inappropriate or incorrect processing strategies is that they feed incorrect L2 linguistic data into their developing systems. Subsequent to the discussion of linguistic items and processing problems, we review the findings relevant to the first major focus of PI research, that is, the effects of PI compared to those of other instruction types. The first question PI researchers addressed was whether PI was effective instruction and if it was better instruction, better than 'traditional' instruction. Do learners who receive PI make greater linguistic gains than learners who receive other types of instruction? After the discussion of PI versus other instruction types we review the findings relevant to the second major focus of PI research, that is, determining the relative contributions to language development of the two elements that comprise PI, explicit information about grammar and SIA. Is explicit information about the grammar necessary for language development? Are structured input activities alone sufficient to cause language development? Finally, we discuss other issues that research on PI has addressed.

The Processing Problems

If a type of instruction does not address a processing problem, then it is not PI; this statement is our tautology. We provide in Table 2.1 an overview of the processing problems that have been addressed by PI research. We refer to the updated and reformulated principles of VanPatten's 2004b work even though the research cited precedes the reformulation and, in fact, contributed to the reformulation. In the sections that follow, we will provide an explanation of the processing problems that PI has addressed.

Table 2.1   Overview of the Processing Problems addressed in PI Research*

Processing Principle VanPatten 2004b	Linguistic Items Investigated	Study
P2. The First Noun Principle. Learners tend to process the first noun or pronoun they encounter in a sentence as the subject/ agent	1. Spanish object pronouns	1. Sanz 1997, 2004; VanPatten & Cadierno 1993; VanPatten & Fernández 2004; VanPatten & Oikennon 1996; VanPatten & Sanz 1995
	2. French causative	2. VanPatten & Wong 2004
P1b. The Lexical Preference Principle. Learners will tend to rely on lexical items as opposed to grammatical form to get meaning when both encode the same semantic information	1. Spanish preterite tense 2. Italian future tense 3. Spanish subjunctive 4. English simple past tense 5. French negation and indefinite articles	1. Cadierno 1995 2. Benati 2001, 2004a 3. Farley 2001, 2004 4. Benati 2005 5. Wong 2004
P1c. The Preference for Non-redundancy Principle. Learners are more likely to process nonredundant meaningful grammatical form before they process redundant meaningful forms.	1. Italian gender agreement with adjectives 2. Spanish subjunctive 3. French negation and indefinite articles	1. Benati 2004b 2. Farley 2001, 2004 3. Wong 2004

Processing Principle VanPatten 2004b	Linguistic Items Investigated	Study
P1d. The Meaning-Before-Nonmeaning Principle. Learners are more likely to process meaningful grammatical forms before nonmeaningful forms irrespective of redundancy.		
Principle 1f. The Sentence Location Principle. Learners tend to process items in sentence initial position before those in final position and those in medial position.	1. Spanish copula 2. Spanish preterite tense 3. Italian future tense 4. Spanish subjunctive 5. English simple past tense	1. Cheng 2002, 2004 2. Cadierno 1995 3. Benati 2001, 2004a 4. Farley 2001, 2004 5. Benati 2005

*A revised version of this table appears in Chapter 6 of this volume so as to include the research presented in Chapters 3, 4 and 5.

P2. The First Noun Principle

VanPatten (1996, 2004b) derived The First Noun Principle from research on both first and second language development with children and adults. Learners pass through a phase of development in which they *tend* [emphasis original] to use word order as a template for assigning the grammatical roles of subject or agent and object. Using this word-order template, learners assign the first noun or pronoun in an utterance the grammatical role of subject or agent. With the subject/agent slot filled, learners then assign other grammatical roles accordingly. The processing problem is quite severe for language acquisition in that the first noun or pronoun is not always the subject/agent as in the case of Spanish object pronouns and French faire-causatif constructions. Learners overwhelmingly misinterpret the following sentence as 'He called María last night.'

> Lo llamó María anoche.
> Him-called-María-last night.
> María called him last night.

The processing error is problematic for communication in that the message is misunderstood. The processing error is problematic for acquisition in that the developing system receives incorrect intake. 'Lo' is an object pronoun not a subject pronoun. As Lee's 2003 critical review demonstrated, learners' use of the First Noun Principle with Spanish object pronouns is so pervasive that under certain linguistic and contextual conditions, fourth-semester learners use it up to 75% of the time to assign grammatical roles and (mis)interpret utterances. Unfortunately for acquisition, the developing system receives a form-meaning mapping that is 75% incorrect!

The French faire-causatif construction presents a similar processing challenge. Learners misinterpret the following sentences to mean 'David washes Jean's car'.

> David fait laver le voiture à Jean.
> David-makes-to wash-the car- to Jean.
> David makes Jean wash the car.

Once again, the processing error is doubly problematic. The communicative intent is misunderstood and the developing system receives incorrect intake. The form-meaning mapping is wrong. Learners do not process two linguistic elements, the verb 'fait' which signals the causative construction and the marker 'à' that signals the agent of the embedded verb. Learners misinterpret the marker 'à' as indicating possession.

The research findings on Spanish object pronouns are extensive as well as consistent and conclusive (Sanz 1997, 2004; VanPatten & Cadierno 1993; VanPatten & Fernández 2004; VanPatten & Oikennon 1996; VanPatten & Sanz 1995). The work on the French causative construction is new but supports the previous findings (VanPatten & Wong 2004). PI is an approach to grammar instruction that has successfully altered learners' tendency to use an incorrect word-order template for assigning grammatical roles.

P1b. The Lexical Preference Principle

VanPatten's (2004b) Lexical Preference Principle states that learners will *tend* [emphasis added] to rely on lexical items as opposed to grammatical form to get meaning when both encode the same semantic information. Let's take tense markers and inflections for example. The semantic information of when something took place or will take place is conveyed with verbal inflections in the following three examples from PI research, Spanish preterite tense (Cadierno, 1995), Italian future tense (Benati, 2001, 2004a), and English simple past tense (Benati, 2005).

> María salió al cine.
> Mario visiterà l'Irlanda del Nord.
> George walked to the store.

The same semantic information of time is also conveyed with adverbials.

> Anoche María salió al cine.
> Domani Mario visiterà l'Irlanda del Nord.
> Last night George walked to the store.

The Lexical Preference Principle accounts for how learners tend to process sentences in which they have multiple cues to meaning; they prefer the lexical items, in this case, the adverbials, and ignore the verbal morphology. The lexemes give the learners the tense; thus, processing the verb morphology becomes unnecessary. This processing strategy is very efficient in terms of allocating resources and, in contrast to the First Noun Principle, accurate in that learners derive the correct semantic information. The acquisitional problem is that the developing system receives nothing with which to construct the L2 linguistic system. In other words, no form-meaning mapping has taken place.

Processing verb tenses is also made difficult by what VanPatten (2004b) terms Principle 1f. The Sentence Location Principle. It states that learners tend to process items in sentence initial position before those in final position and those in medial position. At the sentence level, these inflected verbs tend to appear in medial position, a position not favoured in processing.

The Lexical Preference Principle was a key concept underlying VanPatten's development of 'structured input', a type of manipulated input. For the sake of language development, the input had to be stripped of all cues to meaning *except* the grammatical cue. Learners would then be forced to process the grammatical cue for its meaning, using it to determine tense, as in the following example where learners select the adverbial that appropriately completes the sentence.

> María salió al cine...
> a. anoche. b. mañana.

PI research on the Lexical Preference Principle has also investigated linguistic items other than verb tense, specifically, Spanish subjunctive mood of doubt

(Farley, 2001, 2004a, 2004b) and French negative sentences (Wong, 2004). These constructions contain lexical elements that trigger the presence of other linguistic elements. In the case of Spanish subjunctive, the matrix clause contains the semantic information of doubt that triggers the subjunctive verb morphology in the dependent clause or affirmation that triggers the indicative verb morphology in the dependent clause.

> Dudo que Juan venga. (venga – subjunctive)
> Es cierto que Juan viene. (viene – indicative)

The verb 'dudo' communicates the semantic information that triggers the subjunctive form venga in the dependent clause. This use of the subjunctive is no more than a grammatical reflex.

French affirmative and negative sentences obviously contrast semantically. Negative sentences contain the lexical items 'ne', placed preverbally, and 'pas', placed postverbally. There is, however, a formal (linguistic) difference between affirmative and negative sentences. Affirmative sentences with the verb *avoir* 'to have' mark the object with an indefinite article whereas negatives mark it with the particle *de* if the word following begins with a consonant or *d'* if the word following begins with a vowel.

> Marie a un chat. versus Marie n'a pas de chat.
> Bill a un oiseau. versus Bill n'a pas d'oiseau.

The processing problem in both Spanish subjunctive and French negative sentences is how to get learners to process the formal linguistic features when the semantic notions are conveyed lexically elsewhere in the sentence. There is an additional processing problem in that the lexical semantic information precedes the formal linguistic feature. As learners parse these sentences they encounter the lexical semantic information first. The lexemes render the formal features redundant and, as formulated in VanPatten's (2004b) P1c. The Preference for Non-Redundancy Principle, learners are more likely to process nonredundant meaningful grammatical form before they process redundant meaningful forms. In the cases of Spanish subjunctive and French negatives, the input cannot be stripped of its lexical indicators as we did with verb tense; the input must be manipulated or structured in other ways. And so, learners were presented with the formal linguistic feature first, and then had to determine the appropriate lexical indicators that would have triggered it.

> ...Juan venga.
> a. Dudo que... b. Es cierto que...

...de camarade de chambre.
a. Luc a... b. Luc n'a pas... c. neither A nor B d. Both A and B

PI is an approach to grammar instruction that has successfully focused learners on grammatical form in order to use it to make a semantically appropriate selection. The research on the Lexical Preference Principle includes work on Spanish, French, Italian and English as second languages. It has explored grammatical forms as diverse as verb tenses, mood distinctions, and negation/affirmation. The work on the Lexical Preference Principle shows us that PI not only corrects inappropriate word order processing strategies, but it also provides learners *new* strategies for processing input.

The Effects of PI, TI and MOI

The effects of PI on second language development have been compared empiri-cally to those of two other types of grammar instruction, traditional instruction (TI) and meaning-based output instruction (MOI). TI and MOI consist of explicit information about a grammatical structure followed by production practices. These production practices for TI can be categorised as mechanical and meaningful drills such as substitution and transformation drills for which there is only one correct answer (Lee and VanPatten, 2003, p. 121). The produc-tion practices for MOI can be categorised as structured output activities (Lee and VanPatten, 2003, p. 173–177).

In Table 2.2 we present a chronological overview of the effects of PI compared to those of TI beginning with VanPatten & Cadierno (1993), the first empirical investigation on PI. The research generated under this focus has investigated different processing problems, including the First Noun Principle, The Lexical Preference Principle, and The Sentence Location Principle in second languages such as Spanish, French, Italian and English. Typically, the researchers evaluate language development using two assess-ment tasks, one that requires learners to interpret utterances and another that requires learners to produce the target form. In their original conception of this research, VanPatten & Cadierno (1993) explained that the two types of tasks paralleled the two treatments. The interpretation task was seen as an extension of the structured input activities whereas the form production task was an extension of the traditional output practices. VanPatten & Cadierno also established the design for all future PI research. That is, they and all others subsequently used a pretest/posttest repeated measures design assess-ing learners' performance on the interpretation task independently of their performance on the production task.

Table 2.2   The Immediate Effects of PI Compared to Those of TI*

Study	Linguistic Item	Interpretation Results	Production Results
VanPatten & Cadierno 1993	Spanish object pronouns	PI > (TI = C)	(PI = TI) > C
Cadierno 1995	Spanish preterite tense	PI > (TI = C)	(PI = TI) > C
Benati 2001	Italian future tense	PI > TI > C	(PI = TI) > C
Cheng 2002	Spanish copula	PI > (TI = C)	(PI = TI) > C
VanPatten & Wong 2004	French causative	PI > TI > C	(PI = TI) > C
Cheng 2004	Spanish copula	--	(PI = TI) > C
Benati 2005	English simple past	PI > TI = MOI	PI = TI = MOI

PI = Processing Instruction
TI = Traditional Instruction
C = Control group
MOI = Meaning-based Output Instruction

*A revised version of this table appears in Chapter 6 of this volume so as to include the research presented in Chapters 3, 4 and 5.

The findings are robust that PI > TI on interpretation tasks. Learners who receive PI score significantly higher on interpretation tasks than learners who receive TI, no matter the target language nor the processing problem addressed. The findings are also robust that PI = TI on form production tasks. Learners who receive PI, during which they never produce a target form, score the same on form production tasks no matter the target language nor the processing problem addressed.

Three of the studies presented in Table 2.3 also investigated the important question of whether the effects of PI on language development were durative or ephemeral. We provide an overview of these works in Table 2.3. The research base comprises studies on Spanish and Italian and has addressed different processing problems: the First Noun Principle (VanPatten & Cadierno, 1993; VanPatten & Wong, 2004); the Sentence Location Principle (Benati, 2001, 2004a; Cadierno 1995; Cheng 2002, 2004); and, the Lexical Preference

Principle (Benati, 2001, 2004a; Cadierno, 1995). The last delayed posttest in two studies took place one month after instruction (Cadierno, 1995; VanPatten & Cadierno, 1993) whereas the delayed posttest took place three weeks after instruction in the other study (Benati, 2001). Based on these results we affirm that the effects of PI on interpretation tasks compared to those of TI are durative. Those learners who receive PI improve significantly on interpreta- tion tasks due to the instructional treatment and retain this knowledge for 3 or 4 weeks (Benati, 2001; Cadierno, 1995; VanPatten & Cadierno, 1993). Learners who received TI either do not improve on the interpretation task (Cadierno, 1995; VanPatten & Cadierno, 1993) or do not improve to the extent PI learners do (Benati, 2001). The findings for the production tasks across the three studies are identical. Learners who receive PI improve on the production tasks to the same degree as learners who receive TI and the effects endure for three or four weeks (Benati, 2001; Cadierno, 1995; VanPatten & Cadierno, 1993).

Table 2.3   The Durative Effects of PI Compared to Those of TI

Study	Linguistic Item	Time	Interpretation Results	Production Results
VanPatten & Cadierno 1993	Spanish object pronouns	T1 = pretest T2 = immediate post test T3 = one week later T4 = one month later	PI > TI PI: T1 < (T2 = T3 = T4) TI: T1 = T2 = T3 = T4	PI = TI PI: T1 < (T2 = T3 = T4) TI: T1 < (T2 = T3 = T4)
Cadierno 1995	Spanish preterite tense	T1 = pretest T2 = immediate post test T3 = one week later T4 = one month later	PI > TI PI: T1 < (T2 = T3 = T4) TI: T1 = T2 = T3 = T4	PI = TI PI: T1 < (T2 = T3 = T4) TI: T1 < (T2 = T3 = T4)

Study	Linguistic Item	Time	Interpretation Results	Production Results
Benati 2001	Italian future tense	T1 = pretest T2 = immediate post test T3 = three weeks later	PI > TI PI: T1 < T2 = T3 TI: T1 < T2 = T3 PI-T2 > TI-T2	PI = TI T1< T2 = T3

PI = Processing Instruction
TI = Traditional Instruction
T1 = Time 1 or pretest
T2 = Time 2 or delayed posttest
T3 = Time 3 or second delayed posttest
T4 = Time 4 or third delayed posttest

The ensuing discussion and debate surrounding the positive effects of PI on interpretation and form production as well as the null effects of TI on interpretation focused on two issues. First, VanPatten & Cadierno (1993) and Cadierno (1995) provided learners two different types of explicit information. The PI group received an explanation of the grammar item as well as information about processing strategies. The TI group only received information about the grammar item. Also, some questioned the form-oriented output practices used in TI even though VanPatten & Cadierno (1993) and Cadierno (1995) adapted them from a widely-used textbook, arguably the most successful Spanish-language textbook ever published in the United States. To address these issues researchers decided to compare the effects of PI to those of MOI, meaning-based output instruction and to provide the same explicit information to all treatment groups. [We note here that Benati (2001) addressed these issues by including meaning-based output practices with his TI and provided all learners the same explicit information.] We present in Table 2.4 an overview of the findings on the effects of PI compared to those of MOI. The number of studies is limited; they do, however, address the processing problems of the Sentence Location Principle, the Lexical Preference Principle and the First Noun Principle (Benati, 2005; Farley, 2001, 2004; Morgan-Short and Bowden 2006).

Table 2.4   The Immediate Effects of PI Compared to Those of MOI*

Study	Linguistic Item	Interpretation	Production
Farley 2001a	Spanish subjunctive N =29	PI > MOI	PI = MOI
Farley 2001b, 2004a	Spanish subjunctive N= 50	PI = MOI	PI = MOI
Benati 2005	English simple past Greek L1	PI > MOI = TI	PI = MOI =TI
	Chinese L1	PI > MOI = TI	PI = MOI =TI
Morgan-Short & Bowden 2006	Spanish object pronouns N=45	PI = MOI > C	PI = MOI MOI > C PI = C

PI = Processing Instruction
TI = Traditional Instruction
MOI = Meaning-based Output Instruction
C = Control Group

*A revised version of this table appears in Chapter 6 of this volume so as to include the research presented in Chapters 3, 4 and 5.

The findings of these studies on learners' performance on form production tasks is perfectly consistent. Learners who receive PI improve to the same extent as those who receive MOI on form production in that there is no significant difference between scores for the PI and MOI groups. The findings of this line of investigation on the interpretation task are not consistent. Those learners who receive PI sometimes score significantly higher on interpretation tasks than those who receive MOI (Benati, 2005; Farley, 2001a) and sometimes make equal gains (Farley, 2001b, 2004; Morgan-Short and Bowden 2006). We return to the issue of the effects of PI versus MOI in Chapter 5 of this book, at which point we present new research that further isolates the exceptional findings (Farley 2001b, 2004; Morgan-Short and Bowden 2006). We note here, though, that Benati's 2005 research represents an important step toward the generalisability of the findings of PI research beyond native speakers of English and beyond Romance languages. (See Lee (2004) for more on the generalisability and limitations of PI research findings.)

As can be seen in Table 2.5, the durative effects of PI are again affirmed by the comparisons of PI with MOI. Learners who receive PI improve significantly on interpretation and production tasks and retain that knowledge for two or three weeks (Farley, 2001a, 2001b, 2004; Morgan-Short & Bowden 2006). An interesting note to the research on MOI is Morgan-Short & Bowden's 2006 finding that the immediate effects of MOI on interpretation and production diminish significantly one week later whereas the effects of PI are consistent. The MOI groups interpretation scores dropped from 71% at Time 2 to 46% at Time 3. Their production scores dropped from 70% at Time 2 to 32% at Time 3.

Table 2.5   The Durative Effects of PI Compared to Those for MOI

Study	Linguistic Item	Time	Interpretation	Production
Farley 2001a	Spanish subjunctive N= 29	T1 = pretest T2 = immediate posttest T3 = two weeks	PI > MOI T1 < (T2 = T3)	PI = MOI T1 < (T2 = T3)
Farley 2001b, 2004a	Spanish subjunctive N=50	T1 = pretest T2 = immediate posttest T3 = two weeks	PI = MOI T1 < (T2 = T3)	PI = MOI T1 < (T2 = T3)
Morgan-Short & Bowden 2006	Spanish object pronouns N=45	T1 = pretest T2 = immediate posttest T3 = one week	PI = MOI T1: PI = MOI = C T2: (PI = MOI) > C T3: (PI > MOI) > C	PI = MOI T1: PI = MOI = C T2: MOI > PI >C T3: (MOI = PI) > C

Study	Linguistic Item	Time	Interpreta-tion	Production
PI = Processing Instruction MOI = Meaning-based Output Instruction C = Control group T1 = Time 1 or pretest T2 = Time 2 or delayed posttest T3 = Time 3 or second delayed posttest T4 = Time 4 or third delayed posttest				

The Relative Effects of the Components of PI (EI and SI)

All descriptions of PI refer to the two elements that comprise it, explicit information or explanation and structured input practices. The explicit information provided learners with an explanation of the grammatical structure as well as information about processing strategies. To provide information about processing strategies as part of grammar instruction was a novel concept. Structured input was also a novel concept. Whereas VanPatten treated structured input as a type of enhanced input (1996), Lee (2000) distinguished it as a new type of input among five (i.e., comprehensible input, simplified input, enhanced input, interactionally-modified input, and structured input). The question arose, then, whether the positive effects of PI were due to this novel type of explicit information or to the novel structured input practices.

Table 2.6   The Relative Effects of The Components of PI Compared to Each Other

Study	Linguistic Item	Interpretation Results	Production Results
VanPatten & Oikennon 1996	Spanish object pronouns	(PI = SI) > EI	(PI = SI) > EI
Benati 2004a	Italian future tense	(PI = SI) > EI	(PI = SI) > EI
Farley 2004b	Spanish subjunctive	PI > SI	PI > SI
Sanz 2004	Spanish object pronouns	SI = SI + EFB	SI = SI + EFB

Study	Linguistic Item	Interpretation Results	Production Results
Wong 2004b	French negative + indefinite article	(PI = SI) > (EI = C)	(PI = SI) > C PI > EI EI = SI EI = C
Benati 2004b	Italian gender agreement on adjectives	(PI = SI) > EI	(PI = SI) > EI

PI = Processing Instruction comprising EI and SI
SI = Structured Input activities only
EI = Explicit Information only
EFB = Explicit Feedback
C = Control group

In four of the five studies, see Table 2.6, to have compared the effects of PI (comprised of EI + SI) to the effects of SI alone and EI alone, the effects of PI and SI alone are equal on both interpretation and production tasks (Benati, 20004a, 2005; VanPatten & Oikennon, 1996; Wong, 2004b). In other words, learners' improvement on the interpretation and production tasks is *caused* by them having performed structured input activities. These results are confirmed for Spanish, French and Italian and on a variety of linguistic items that represent various processing problems. The addition of explicit grammatical information in the PI treatment did not cause greater improvement. Sanz (2004) provides another bit of evidence for how great the effects of structured input activities are. She compared the effects of learners performing SI activities only to those of learners performing the SI activities plus receiving explicit feedback on their wrong answers. She found no significant differences in the two groups of learners' scores on either an interpretation or production task. The stand-alone finding is Farley's (2004); the effects of PI are significantly greater than the effects of SI alone. He attributes this finding to the complexity of the linguistic item he investigated, the Spanish subjunctive. The new research we present in Chapter 5 on Italian and French subjunctive will question this assertion.

Table 2.7   The Durative Effects of The Components of PI Compared to Each Other

Study	Linguistic Item	Time	Interpretation Results	Production Results
Benati 2004a	Italian future tense	T1 = pretest T2 = immediate posttest T3 = one month	(PI = SI) > EI PI: T1 < (T2 = T3) SI: T1 < (T2 = T3) EI: T1 < (T2 = T3)	(PI = SI) > EI PI: T1 < (T2 = T3) SI: T1 < (T2 = T3) EI: T1 < (T2 = T3)
Farley 2004	Spanish subjunctive	T1 = pretest T2 = immediate posttest T3 = two weeks	PI > SI PI: T1 < (T2 = T3) SI: T1 < (T2 = T3)	PI > SI PI: T1 < (T2 = T3) SI: T1 < (T2 = T3)

PI = Processing Instruction comprising EI and SI
SI = Structured Input activities only
EI = Explicit Information only
T1 = Time 1 or pretest
T2 = Time 2 or delayed posttest
T3 = Time 3 or second delayed posttest

We have but two studies that examined the relative durative effects of the components of PI (Benati, 2004a; Farley, 2004b). Whereas Benati (2004a) found that the effects of PI equalled those of SI, Farley found that the effects of PI were greater than those of SI. In both studies the directionality of the durative effects of PI and SI only were the same. Both PI and SI yielded a significant and sustained improvement in performance on interpretation and production tasks.

Other Issues

Previous research on the effects of PI has sought to illuminate two other issues, long term effects of PI instruction and task effects. We have, to this point, only referred to the durative effects of PI. We chose the term durative to reflect the fact that measuring the effects of a treatment one week, two weeks, three or four weeks later does not constitute a truly longitudinal investigation. VanPatten & Fernández (2004) however, controlled a curriculum so that learners received no further instruction in the targeted linguistic item (Spanish object pronouns). They tracked learners eight months after receiving their one and only PI treatment. They compared the results of the pretests (interpretation and production) with the 8-month-delayed posttests and found that learners' scores were significantly higher on the delayed posttests than on the pretests. These delayed posttest scores were, however, significantly lower than those on the immediate posttest. There are, then, long term yet diminished effects for PI.

Sanz (1997) addressed the issue of the assessment tasks used in PI research. As has been clear in this review, the type of production task that has been used in the prototypical PI research is a sentence-level form production task. Sanz expanded on this approach by assessing the effects of PI on Spanish object pronouns by manipulating mode (oral versus written) as well as task (sentence completion and video retelling). From pretest to immediate posttest, learners made significant improvement on oral and written sentence completion and written video retelling. Even though they improved from 9% to 26% on oral video retelling, the difference was not statistically significant.

Conclusions

PI is a very effective approach to grammar instruction in that it has never failed to yield significant improvement in learner performance on either interpretation or form production tasks. When presented with a processing problem in the L2, learners can be taught to alter their processing strategies thereby delivering better intake (i.e., grammatically richer) to their developing systems. This better intake yields improved performance on both interpretation and production tasks. PI comprises explicit information about a grammatical form as well as information about processing strategies and structured input activities. The evidence leans heavily toward concluding that the SI activities cause the improvement in learners' performance. The effects of PI as well as SI are durative in the short term (one month) and are still in evidence after 8 months although the effects are diminished with time.

3 The effects of structured input activities on the acquisition of two Japanese linguistic features

Background

The main objective of PI is to help learners to circumvent their ineffective and/or inaccurate default strategies and to push them to rely exclusively on forms or structures to derive meaning from input. As Wong (2004a: 35) states it, PI 'pushes learners to abandon their inefficient processing strategies for more optimal ones so that better form-meaning connections are made'. As discussed in Chapter 1, in order to achieve this goal PI must provide learners with a type of practice called structured input activities (SI henceforth), designed to force learners to process the target form in the input and at the same time help them to make better form-meaning connections. VanPatten has suggested (VanPatten 1996; 2002) that PI provides more effective practice than traditional instruction (TI) as it equips learners with the tools to convert input into intake. Clearly our review of the literature in Chapter 2 affirms this statement.

The general findings of studies measuring the effects of PI (see for a full review VanPatten, 2002; Lee, 2004; and Chapter 2 in this book) versus traditional output-based instruction show that learners receiving PI seem to benefit in their ability to process input (interpretation tasks) as well as being able to access the target feature when performing production tasks. The next question raised concerning the results of PI studies was to determine what factors within the PI approach are responsible for the beneficial effect of this form of grammatical intervention. What are the relative contributions to language development of the two elements that comprise PI, explicit information about grammar and structured input activities.

VanPatten and Oikennon (1996) were the first who sought to address this question by measuring the effects of the two main components of PI: explicit information and SI practice. As reviewed in Chapter 2 the result of this first study showed that the positive effects of PI are due to SI practice and not the explicit information component. In an attempt to generalise the findings of this first study a series of conceptual replications have been conducted. On the one hand, the majority of these studies (Benati 2004a, 2004b; Wong 2004b), have produced similar results to those of VanPatten & Oikkenon (1996). The main findings from these empirical studies confirm that SI practice is the causative variable responsible for learners improved performance. While SI practice seems to play the pivotal role, explicit information seems to be unnecessary and have no impact on helping learners to interpret or produce sentences using the target language. On the other hand, another set of results (Farley 2004b) seems to indicate that the explicit information component in PI might have a beneficial effect in helping learners firstly to notice and subsequently to process forms or structures. Although, the majority of studies which have teased the effects of the main components of PI have overall underscored that it is the SI component in PI that is responsible for learners' improved performance, it is necessary to conduct more research in order to generalise those findings. As shown in Tables 2.6 and 2.7, the research conducted to date on this issue has focused exclusively on Romance languages. Will the results be similar for other language types?

Motivation of the study

Previous research affirms that learners' strategies for processing input can be altered through SI. The present study continues in this vein. The main purpose of the present study is to compare the relative effects of SI with those of TI on the acquisition of a non-Romance L2, namely, Japanese. SI practice is used as a form of intervention on two different linguistic feature of Japanese and relative processing problems. In this sense an additional aim for this study is to establish whether or not there are cumulative effects for the SI practice. As stated by Lee (2004) 'to date, each PI intervention has been carried out in isolation, that is, one set of learners is taught a word-order processing strategy, another set a perceptual processing strategy, and yet another a semantic processing strategy. What are the cumulative effects of receiving PI instruction on different types of strategies?' (p.320).

The specific aims of the present study are threefold. We aim to collect empirical evidence to verify the generalisability of SI to a different language (acquisition of Japanese past forms and affirmative vs. negative present forms). We explore the effects of instruction on two different processing problems (The Lexical Preference Principle, P1 b., and The Sentence Location Principle, P1 d.). And, finally, we seek to observe possible cumulative effects for SI practice.

Research Questions

In order to address the questions raised in this study we decided to compare SI practice to TI as Japanese is often taught in a very traditional way. The specific research questions for this study were:

Q1. Will there be any differences in how two groups of learners of Japanese exposed to two different types instructional treatments (SI vs. TI) interpret and produce sentences containing and expressing positive or negative present tense forms?

Q2. Will there be any differences in how two groups of learners of Japanese exposed to two different types instructional treatments (SI vs. TI) interpret and produce sentences containing and expressing past tense forms?

Design

Participants and procedure

Participants in the present study were beginning level students of Japanese. All subjects were adult native speakers of Italian and were studying Japanese in a private school in Italy. They received 2 hours of instruction per day, over two consecutive days. Forty four subjects were reduced to 27 (final data pool) as participants went through a series of filters (e.g., subjects with previous knowledge in the two targeted linguistic features were not included in the final pool). Additionally, participants who scored more than 60% on the pre-tests were not included in the final data pool. Participants were randomly assigned to the two groups and the final sizes were 13 for the SI group and 14 for the TI group.

We adopted a pretest/posttest approach to examine the short term effects of the two instructional treatments. We administered pretests to the subjects before the beginning of the instructional treatment and post-tests immediately after the end of the instructional treatment (see Table 3.1 for an overview of the experimental design).

Table 3.1   Overview of the experiment

RANDOM PROCEDURE/ PRE –TEST	INSTRUCTIONAL PERIOD	POST-TESTS
↓	↓	↓
Two Groups formed SI *n* = 13 TI *n* = 14	Two consecutive days (4 hours instruction)	Interpretation & Production
Pre-tests administered: Interpretation & Production		

The two groups received the same type of instruction prior the beginning of the instructional period (e.g. same materials, textbooks, syllabus and exams). The same instructor, who was not the researcher but was the regular instructor, taught both groups during the period of research-based instruction. The instructor was trained by the researcher to act as a facilitator during the experiment. Learners received the instructional treatments (4 hours) on the use of positive and negative present tense forms in Japanese first and then, one week later, they received the same instructional treatments (4 hours) on the second linguistic feature (use of past forms in Japanese). All testing and instruction took place in students' regular classroom.

Grammatical features

We selected the grammatical features of past forms and affirmative and negative present forms in Japanese because of the processing problems each presents to learners. The 'Lexical Preference Principle' (P1 b.) has been investigated in many PI studies (e.g. Cadierno, 1995; Benati, 2001; Benati and Paula Romero-Lopez, 2003; Benati 2004b; see also Benati, VanPatten, Wong, 2005; Romero-López, 2002). In a sentence such as *Kino kaisha ni ikimashita* (Yesterday, I went to the office) both the lexical item *kaisha* and the verb ending *mashita* communicate past tense. According to the 'Lexical Preference Principle' learners will naturally tend to rely on the lexical item over the redundant verb inflection in order to gather semantic information. The main purpose of SI in this study, then, is to push learners to process the past tense marker that otherwise may not be processed as learners do not need to process it to assign pastness to the meaning of the sentence.

We chose the positive and negative present tense forms in Japanese because they test the Sentence Location Principle (P1 d.). According to VanPatten (2002) learners tend to process items in sentence initial position before those in final position and those in medial position. This processing strategy has been investigated in previous studies (Farley, 2001a; 2001b; Benati, 2005; see also Benati, VanPatten, Wong, 2005) and SI has proved vital in helping learners to alter this processing problem. Japanese sentences end with verbs and the ending of the verb encodes the tense as well as marks the sentence meaning as positive or negative. Because learners tend to process elements in the initial position before elements in the final position, they would skip over the grammatical marker and find difficult to establish whether the sentence is positive or negative. We designed SIA activities to push learners to process the element in final position that otherwise may not be processed and would lead to misinterpretation of the sentence.

Instructional treatments

We designed two separate packets of materials, one for the SI group and another for the TI group. Instructional materials were balanced in all respects (e.g. vocabulary, total number of activities) but differed fundamentally in one requiring learners to process input and the other requiring them to produce output. In addition the TI group received explicit information about the two linguistic features during the instructional treatment. The instructional treatment for the TI group consisted of explicit information about the form and output practice, whereas the SI group did not receive explicit information. They practiced processing input sentences. The TI activities (mechanical in nature) required the subjects to produce accurately past forms and present forms in positive and negative sentences. The SI practices, however, required learners to make appropriate form-meaning connections.

SI

This input-based treatment consisted of the use of SIA activities (referential and affective types) in which learners have to respond to the content of sentences. We include two SIA activities in Appendix A and another two in Appendix B for the two linguistic items investigated. We used two formats for the activities: matching and binary options (Lee & VanPatten 2003). Students in the SI group never produced a sentence containing the targeted linguistic features. The activities engaged them in processing input sentences. They had to comprehend and interpret them so that they could make better form-meaning connections. In both grammatical items the input was 'structured' so that learners had to attend to the form to complete the task. They had to connect the grammatical form to its the meaning. As can be seen in our appended activities, we did not include any temporal adverbs in the SI practices. Learners could only use verbal morphology as the indicator of tense since we did not include any lexical indicators of tense. Learners had to look to sentence final position to find the morphology rather than rely on what appears in sentence initial position.

TI

We prepared the second set of materials for the TI treatment to conform with more traditional grammar instruction. This output-based treatment had the following characteristics. Learners first encountered the presentation and explanation of forms. We provide the explanations in Appendices C and D. Following the explanations, learners found output practices for which they had to produce the correct forms. We provide sample activities in Appendices C and D. We constructed all the activities so that learners produced the forms at sentence level. Some of the TI practice activities lacked any referential meaning as is the nature of some traditional output practices.

Assessment

We produced two tests for each linguistic feature: one for the interpretation tasks and one for the production tasks. We provide the tests in Appendices E and F. In that we assess both interpretation and production, our assessments favour neither instructional group. An interpretation task was used as a measure of knowledge gained at interpreting past tense forms at sentence level. In the case of the use of past forms the interpretation test consisted of twenty aural sentences (ten in the present which served as distracters and ten targets in the past). None contained temporal adverbs nor subject nouns or pronouns so that the participants could not rely on these elements to assign tense. They had to focus on verb morphology as the only indicator to establish when the action was taking place (present vs. past). Subjects were asked to establish whether the sentence expressed an action which was taking place now or in the past.

The second interpretation test constructed for the second linguistic feature also consisted of 20 sentences (five affirmative, five negative, and 10 distracters in a different tense). Participants had to rely on the verb (in final position) to establish whether the sentence was in the present negative or affirmative forms. If they were not sure they could chose the 'not sure' (warikasen) option.

The tests were recorded and presented to the subjects on a tape player. Each item was played once with no repetition so that the test would measure real-time comprehension. The pre and post-tests were balanced in terms of difficulty and vocabulary. In the interpretation tasks the raw scores were calculated as follows: incorrect response = 0 point, correct response = 1point. In the first study only the past sentences were counted. The maximum possible score was 10. In the second study only the present affirmative or negative correct responses received 1 point.

We developed sentence-completion production tasks to measure learner's ability to produce correct forms. In the case of the positive vs. negative present forms the written production grammar test consisted of ten sentences to complete (five affirmative and five negative) in the present form. In the written production tasks for past tense forms learners supplied the correct past tense forms in Japanese. The scoring procedure was the same for both written tasks with a maximum score of ten points. In both production tasks we scored a fully correct form as 1 point and gave no points to a form that was not fully correct.

Results

Japanese affirmative vs. negative present tense

The interpretation data

In order to determine that all subjects were at the same level prior to receiving the instructional treatments, we compared their scores on the pretest. We conducted a one-way ANOVA on the pre-test scores alone. It revealed no significant differences among the two groups' means before instruction ($p= .920$). We will attribute any differences we find after instruction to the effects of the treatments.

The means are presented in Table 3.2 and graphically displayed in Graph 3.1. We used a repeated measures ANOVA on the raw scores of the interpretation tests. The results of the ANOVA revealed a significant main effect for instruction Treatment ($F(1,27) = 117.466$, $p = .000$) and for Time $F(1,27) = 260.339$, $p = .000$), as well as a significant interaction between Treatment and Time ($F(1,27) = 156.086$, $p = .000$). These results reveal that SI activities cause a significant improvement in interpreting forms and meanings but TI does not.

Table 3.2   Means and standard deviation for Interpretation task pre-test and post-test for Japanese affirmative and negative present tense

		Pre-test		Post-test 1	
Variable	n	Mean	SD	Mean	SD
SI	13	.634	.650	6.23	.832
TI	14	.642	.745	1.36	.842

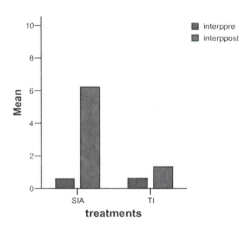

Figure 3.1 Means by instructional treatment for interpretation task (pre-test and post-test) for Japanese affirmative and negative present tense

The production data

In order to determine that all subjects were at the same level prior to receiving the instructional treatments, we compared their scores on the production pretest. We conducted a one-way ANOVA on the pre-test scores alone. The one-way ANOVA conducted on the pre-test showed no statistically significant difference between the groups ($p = .886$) for the written task. We will attribute any differences we find after instruction to the effects of the treatments. We present the means for the pretests and posttests in Table 3.3.

A repeated measures ANOVA was performed to establish the effects of SI practices and TI on the way learners produce written sentences to express past meaning. The results of the ANOVA indicated no significant main effect for Instruction ($F (1,27) = .138, p = .713$) and no significant interaction between Instruction and Time ($F(1,27) = .335, p = .568$). However, the statistical analysis showed a significant effect for Time ($F (1,27) =655.942, p = .000$). These results reveal that both groups made significant gains in producing forms and that neither group was superior to the other.

Table 3.3   Means and standard deviation for Production task pre-test and post-test for Japanese affirmative and negative present tense

		Pre-test		Post-test 1	
Variable	n	Mean	SD	Mean	SD
SI	13	.4615	.519	5.92	.641
TI	14	.4329	.646	6.14	1.351

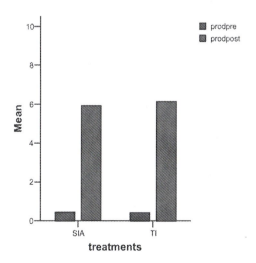

Figure 3.2   Means by instructional treatment for production task (pre-test and post-test) for Japanese affirmative and negative present tense

Japanese past tense

The interpretation data

In order to determine that all subjects were at the same level prior to receiving the instructional treatments, we compared their scores on the interpretation pretest. We conducted a one-way ANOVA on the pre-test scores alone. The one-way ANOVA conducted on the pre-test showed no statistically significant difference between the groups' scores ($p = .414$) for the task. We will attribute any differences we find after instruction to the effects of the treatments. We present the means for the pretests and posttests in Table 3.4 and in Graph 3.3.

Table 3.4   Means and standard deviation for Interpretation task pre-test and post-test for Japanese past tense

		Pre-test		Post-test 1	
Variable	n	Mean	SD	Mean	SD
SI	13	.62	.650	7.38	.916
TI	14	.43	.514	1.21	.893

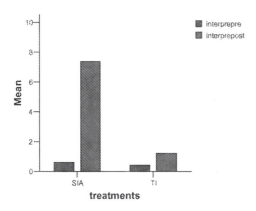

Figure 3.3 Means by instructional treatment for interpretation task (pre-test and post-test) for Japanese past tense

We used a repeated measures ANOVA on the raw scores of the interpretation task to establish the possible effects of instruction on the way learners interpret sentences where the past tense is only expressed by verb morphology. The results showed that there were significant main effects for Instruction $F(1,27) = 250.250, p = .000$) and Time $F(1,27) = 294.462, p = .000$) as well as a significant for interaction between Instruction and Time $F(1,27) = 184.706, p = .000$). The means in Table 3.4 indicate that the SI group made greater gains than the TI group. Performing SI activities and practices had a positive and statistically significant effect on how participants interpreted sentences containing the Japanese past tense.

The production data

In order to determine that all subjects were at the same level prior to receiving the instructional treatments, we compared their scores on the production pretest. We conducted a one-way ANOVA on the pre-test scores alone. The one-way ANOVA conducted on the pre-test scores showed no statistically significant difference between the groups ($p = .166$) for the written task. We will attribute any differences we find after instruction to the effects of the treatments. We present the means for the pretests and posttests in Table 3.5.

We performed a repeated measures ANOVA used to establish the possible effects of SI activities and TI on the way learners produce written sentences to express past meaning in Japanese. The results indicated no significant main effect for Instruction (F $(1,27) = 1.130, p = .290$), but a significant effect for Time $F(1,27) = 428.401, p = .001$). There was no significant interaction between Instruction and Time ($F(1,27) = .234, p = .663$). The effect for Time shows us that both groups significantly improved equally their production of forms.

Table 3.5   Means and standard deviation for Production task pre-test and post-test for Japanese past tense

		Pre-test		Post-test 1	
Variable	n	Mean	SD	Mean	SD
SI	13	.4615	.66023	6.0	1.08012
TI	14	.6667	.73380	6.0741	1.10683

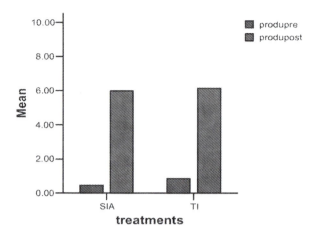

Figure 3.4 Means by instructional treatment for production task (pre-test and post-test) for Japanese past tense

Summary of results

Based on previous research we hypothesised (Q1. and Q2.) that the groups who carried out SI activities would perform better than the TI groups on the interpretation tasks on both linguistic features of Japanese, i.e., affirmative and negative present tense and past tense. The statistical results confirm our hypothesis and contribute to the growing body of research on this topic.

The results from this study also revealed that (Q3.) instruction on the first perceptual processing principle received by the SI group might have helped learners in this group to pick up the second perceptual strategy more quickly and efficiently as their performance in both interpretation and production tasks in the second linguistic feature improved (see the means table of the two consecutive classroom experiments, and also see Tables 3.6 and 3.7 for a summary of the two-way ANOVA).

Table 3.6   Summary of results of the ANOVAs for Japanese affirmative and negative present tense

Data	df	SS	MS	F	p
Interpretation					
Instruction	1	79.154	79.154	117.466	.000 *
Time	1	135.033	135.033	260.339	.000 *
Time x Instruction	1	80.959	80.959	156.086	.000 *
Production					
Instruction	1	.118	.118	655.942	.713
Time	1	420.956	420.956	.335	.000 *
Time x Instruction	1	.215	.215	.335	.568

*significant

Table 3.7   Summary of the results of the ANOVAs for Japanese past tense

Data	df	SS	MS	F	p
Interpretation					
Instruction	1	136.208	136.208	250.250	.000 *
Time	1	192.371	192.371	294.462	.000 *
Time x Instruction	1	120.688	120.688	184.706	.000 *
Production					
Instruction	1	.997	.997	1.130	.290
Time	1	394.882	394.882	428.401.	.001 *
Time x Instruction	1	.215	.215	.234	.663

Discussion and Conclusion

We conducted our investigation on native speakers of Italian learning Japanese at a private school in Italy. Our results mirror those of the vast majority of PI research. The learners who carried out structured input activities significantly improved on both interpretation and production tasks whereas those who receive traditional explanation followed by output practices significantly improved only on production tasks but not on interpretation tasks. We found these results for two linguistic features of Japanese, present and past tenses. We underscore the effects on production of carrying out SI practices because these learners never produced a target form in the practice activities.

The results of the research presented in this chapter are very important in that they address key concerns about the generalisability of Processing Instruction. As Lee (2004) pointed out, research on non-Romance languages was a critical area in need of exploration. Our investigation of two linguistic features of Japanese, present and past tenses, have provided the foundation for generalising the results of PI beyond Romance languages. Our results also lend support to one of Lee's (2004) hypotheses; learners of any language should benefit from PI when a language-specific processing problem has been identified.

Our results contribute to the continuing discussion of the crucial role that input processing plays in second language acquisition. Providing input, specifically structured input, pushed learners to successfully process grammatical forms in the input by providing them appropriate processing strategies. In other words, the manipulation of input through SI helped learners to make better form-meaning connections and thus provide grammatically richer intake to the developing system.

Given our results, we suggest that SI is a better instructional intervention than TI. As we pointed out in Chapter 2, with SI you get two benefits: interpretation and production. Our results also show that explicit information is not as beneficial to learners as is input-based practice. Our SI groups did not receive explicit information on the forms or on how to process forms, yet through SI practices they learn to make form-meaning connections. It is the nature of SI practice that has caused changes in learner performance (VanPatten, 2002). In this respect, the results of the present study offer further support for current models of SLA that link input processing and the developing system (VanPatten, 1996, 2002, 2004a, 2004b).

Research on PI has clearly indicated that this input based approach offer more instructional benefits that output practice. Lee and VanPatten (1995: 95) have rightly argued that 'traditional instruction which is intended to cause a change in the developing system, is akin to putting the cart before the horse when it comes to acquisition; the learner is asked to produce when the developing system has not yet had a chance to build up a representation of the language based on input data'. Output practice is not necessary for language development but input practice is. In this sense, our study supports the view that in language teaching input practice should precede output practice. Finally, our results suggest that Japanese language instruction would benefit from incorporating input practices into textbooks and move away from the traditional materials we used in the present study.

Despite the positive outcomes in both investigations, we recognise certain limitations in our study. We acknowledge that a small number of subjects took part in the two experiments. Further research could replicate the study with a larger population. A second limitation is that we measured instructional effects with an immediate post-test battery only. Hence, the durative and longer-term effects of PI were left unexplored. Given the previous research on PI we hypothesise that future research will uphold the durative effects of our findings. We recommend that further research be carried out examining the effects of PI and SI in the acquisition of different linguistic features in Japanese. Our study is a first step in expanding the data base beyond Romance languages that supports the importance of input processing in language development.

Appendix A: SI for past tense

Attività A

Ascolta e determina se l'azione è passata (passato) o si riferisce ad una azione abituale nel presente. Presta attenzione al verbo in posizione finale!

	Kinō	Mainichi
1.	□	□
2.	□	□
3.	□	□
4.	□	□
5.	□	□

Sentence heard by learner:

1. *Kyoto ni ikimashita*
2. *Kaisha ni ikimasu*
3. *Marason o shimashita*
4. *Totemo ii hon o yomimashita*
5. *Gekijyou ni ikimasu*

Attività B

Ascolta le frasi e selezione l'avverbio temporale che si adatta alla frase! .

1. Kinō □   Mainichi □   Maiasa □
2. Kinō □   Mainichi □   Maiasa □
3. Kinō □   Mainichi □   Maiasa □
4. Kinō □   Mainichi □   Maiasa □
5. Kinō □   Mainichi □   Maiasa □

Sentence heard by learner:

1. *Kasha ni ikimashita*
2. *Osoku made nemasu*
3. *Resutoran de hatarakimashita*
4. *Pabu de tomodachi to biiru o nomimasu*
5. *Bar de wain o takusan nomimashita*

Appendix B: SI for affirmative vs. negative in present tense forms

Attività A

Ascolta e determina se la frase è affermativa o negativa. Presta attenzione al verbo in posizione finale!

	Koutei	Hitei
1.	□	□
2.	□	□
3.	□	□
4.	□	□
5.	□	□

Sentence heard by learner:

1. *Watashi wa italiago o benkyou shimasu*
2. *Watashi wa italiago o benkyou shimasen*
3. *Watashi wa London mi sumimasu*
4. *Watashi wa London ni sumimasen*
5. *Watashi wa gekijyou ni ikimasen*

Attività B

Ascolta le frasi riguardo alle abitudini di uno studente. Decidi se sono affirmative o negative e poi stabilisci se sei in accordo o in disaccordo.

	Koutei	Hitei	Hai	Iie
1.	☐	☐		
2.	☐	☐		
3.	☐	☐		
4.	☐	☐		
5.	☐	☐		

Sentence heard by learner:

1. *Watashi wa tomodachi to dekakemasu*
2. *Watashi wa tomodachi to dekakemasen*
3. *Watashi wa gekijyou ni ikimasu*
4. *Watashi wa John to hanashimasen*

Appendix C: Explicit information and output practice for TI – past tense

Il passato si forma con il suffisso *–mashita* (differente dal presente *-masu*) Memorizza i seguenti verbi al passato.

Forme al passato
Ikimashita (andato)
Kimashita (venuto)
Kaerimashita (ritornato)
Mimamishita (visto)
Kikimashita (ascoltato)
Tabemashita (mangiato)
Nonimashita (bevuto)
Kaimashita (comprato)
Yomimashita (letto)
Shimashita (studiato)

Attività A

Trasforma le frasi dall'italiano al giapponese.

1) L'anno scorso sono andato in Italia
2) Ieri sono andato al parco con Paolo
3) La settimana scorso ho corso la maratona
4) Ieri sono andato al cimema
5) Ieri sono andato a teatro con John

Attività B

Cambia le seguenti frasi dal presente al passato.

1) Watashi wa maitoshi Italia ni ikimasu
2) Watashi wa de wain o takusan nomimasu
3) Watashi wa marason o shimasu
4) Watashi wa terebi de tomemo ii eiga o mimasu
5) Watashi wa san-jj ni basu ni norimasu

Appendix D: Explicit information and output practice for TI – affirmative vs. negative in present tense forms

Il presente in frase affermativa si forma con il suffisso *–masu* mentre in frase negative con il suffisso *-masen*). Memorizza i seguenti verbi al presente (forme positive e negative)

Forme del presente	
Affermativa	**Negativa**
Ikimasu (vado)	ikimasen (non vado)
Kimasu (vengo)	kimasen (non vengo)
Kaerimasu (ritorno)	kaerimasen (non ritorno)
Mimasu (vedo)	mimasen (non vedo)
Kikimasu (ascolto)	kikimasen (non acolto)
Tabemasu (mangio)	tabemasen (non mangio)
Nonimasu (bevo)	nominasen (non bevo)
Kaimasu (compro)	kaimasen (non compro)
Yomimasu (leggo)	yominasen (non leggo)
Shimasu (studio)	shimasen (non studio)

Attività A

Trasforma le frasi dall'italiano al giapponese secondo l'esempio:

Io gioco a tennis/ Io non gioco a tennis
watashi wa tenisu o shimasu
watashi wa tenisu o shimasen

1. Io torno a casa presto/ Io non torno a casa presto
2. Io parlo il giapponese/Io non parlo il giapponese
3. Io guaro la TV/ Io non guardo la TV
4. Io ascolto la radio/ Io non ascolto la radio
5. Io prendo l'autobus alle 3/ Io non prendo l'autobus alle tre

Attività B

Cambia le frasi dall'affermativa alla negativa

1) Watashi wa John to hanashimasu
2) Watashi wa nihongo de shimbum o yomimasu
3) Watashi wa gimu ni ikimasu
4) Watashi wa gengogaku o benkyou shimasu
5) Watashi wa ronbun o kakimasu

Appendix E: Assessment tasks for the past tense

Interpretation task (sample)

Ascolta le frasi e stabilisci quando avviene l'azione

1	❑ Kyonen	❑ Maitoshi
2	❑ Kyonen	❑ Maitoshi
3	❑ Kinō	❑ Mainichi
4	❑ Kinō	❑ Mainichi
5	❑ Kinō	❑ Maiban
6	❑ Kinō	❑ Maiban
7	❑ Sakuban	❑ Mainichi

8	❑ Sakuban	❑ Mainichi
9	❑ Kinō	❑ Mainichi
10	❑ Kynō	❑ Mainichi
11	❑ Kyonen	❑ Maitoshi
12	❑ Kyonen	❑ Maitoshi
13	❑ Kinō	❑ Mainichi
14	❑ Kinō	❑ Mainichi
15	❑ Kinō	❑ Maiban
16	❑ Kinō	❑ Maiban
17	❑ Sakuban	❑ Mainichi
18	❑ Sakuban	❑ Mainichi
19	❑ Kinō	❑ Mainichi
20	❑ Kynō	❑ Mainichi

Sentence heard by learner:

1. *italia ni ikimashita*
2. *italia ni ikimasu*
3. *tenisu o shimashita*
4. *tenisu o shimasu*
5. *ii eiga o mimashita*
6. *terebi o mimasu*
7. *osoku made netemashita*
8. *osoku made nemasu*
9. *de Paul to hanashimashita*
10. *de Paul to hanashimasu*
11. *gekijyou ni ikimashita*
12. *no shumatsu tomodachi to sugoshimashita*
13. *restouran de hatarakimasu*
14. *John to kouen o arukimashita*
15. *gakkou de nihongo o benkyou shimashita*
16. *marason o shimashita*
17. *totemo ii hon o yomimashu*

    18. Paul to kouen o arukimashu
    19. Jon to honashimasu
    20. uchi/ie ni kaeriimasu

Production task

Completa le seguenti frasi al passato

1   Kinō sakuban osoku made ————-(dormito).

2   Kinō isshukan mae denwa de Paul to ————-(parlato).

3   Kinō rajio o ————-(ascoltato).

4   Kinō tenisu o ————-(giocato).

5   Kinō italiago o benkyou ————-(studiato).

6   Kinō terebi o ————-(guardato).

7   Kinō italia ni ————-(andato).

8   Kinō rajio o ————-(studiato).

9   Kinō italiago o ————-(insegnato).

10   Kinō totemo osuku ni ————-(andato a letto).

Appendix F: Assessment tasks for the affirmative vs. negative present tense

Interpretation task (sample)

Ascolta le frasi riguardo alle abitudini di uno studente e stabilisci se si tratta di una frase affermativa o positiva al presente.

1	❑ Koutei	❑ Hitei	❑ Wakarimasen
2	❑ Koutei	❑ Hitei	❑ Wakarimasen
3	❑ Koutei	❑ Hitei	❑ Wakarimasen
4	❑ Koutei	❑ Hitei	❑ Wakarimasen
5	❑ Koutei	❑ Hitei	❑ Wakarimasen

6	❏ Koutei	❏ Hitei	❏ Wakarimasen
7	❏ Koutei	❏ Hitei	❏ Wakarimasen
8	❏ Koutei	❏ Hitei	❏ Wakarimasen
9	❏ Koutei	❏ Hitei	❏ Wakarimasen
10	❏ Koutei	❏ Hitei	❏ Wakarimasen
11	❏ Koutei	❏ Hitei	❏ Wakarimasen
12	❏ Koutei	❏ Hitei	❏ Wakarimasen
13	❏ Koutei	❏ Hitei	❏ Wakarimasen
14	❏ Koutei	❏ Hitei	❏ Wakarimasen
15	❏ Koutei	❏ Hitei	❏ Wakarimasen
16	❏ Koutei	❏ Hitei	❏ Wakarimasen
17	❏ Koutei	❏ Hitei	❏ Wakarimasen
18	❏ Koutei	❏ Hitei	❏ Wakarimasen
19	❏ Koutei	❏ Hitei	❏ Wakarimasen
20	❏ Koutei	❏ Hitei	❏ Wakarimasen

Sentence heard by learner:

1. *Watashi wa tomodachi to dekakemasu*
2. *Watashi wa tomodachi to dekakemasen*
3. *no shumatsu tomodachi to sugoshimashita*
4. *Watashi wa terebi o mimasen*
5. *totemo ii hon o yomishamita*
6. *Joan to gekijyou ni ikimashita*
7. *wa terebi o mimasu*
8. *ronbun o kakimashita*
9. *nohongo de shinbun o yomimasen*
10. *uchi/ie ni kaerimashita*
11. *san-ji ni basu ni norimasen*
12. *uchi/ie ni kaerimashita*
13. *watashi wa Alessandro to hanashimasu*
14. *Bernie to hanashimashita*

15. *watashi wa gimu ni ikimasen*
16. *watashi wa gimu ni ikimashita*
17. *watashi wa gekijyou ni ikimasu*
18. *Kinou watashi wa john to kouen a arukimashita*
19. *gengogaku o benkyou shimasu*
20. *bar de wain o takusan*

Production task

Completa le seguenti frasi al presente

1. Watashi wa Italia ni ————-(vado).

2. Watashi wa Italia ni————-(non vado).

3. Watashi wa mainichi tenisu o ————-(gioco).

4. Watashi wa mainichi tenisu o ————-(non gioco).

5. Watashi wa maiban tereibi o————-(non guardo).

6. Watashi wa denwa de Paul to————-(parlo).

7. Watashi wa denwa de Paul to ————-(non parlo).

8. Watashi wa mainichi osoku made————-(dormo).

9. Watashi wa rajio o————-(ascolto).

10. Watashi wa rajio o ————-(non ascolto).

4 Comparing three modes of delivering Processing Instruction on preterite/imperfect distinction and negative informal commands in Spanish

With Jorge Aguilar-Sánchez and Erin M. McNulty

Language instruction, as is true of many fields, is always searching for the 'next big thing', the method, approach, procedures or practices that will help students to learn faster and retain longer. We speak of helping students to learn rather than causing learning to happen because we have long recognised the validity of Stevick's (1976) discussion of the relationship between meaning and memory; some students learn what they are taught and others do not because learning does not so much result from, as interacts with, teaching. But what we have learned from the research on PI is that some teaching is, in and of itself, more effective than others.

The findings from research on second language acquisition focused attention on learning processes, those mental activities taking place in learners' heads. We described, as best we could, how learners took the input they were exposed to and created a second language grammar or developing system for themselves. How learners processed input and what input became intake became major research foci and major points of theoretical debate. Those researchers who examined classroom learners were also interested in extrapolating the pedagogical implications of their work. And so, from VanPatten's research on and theorising about input processing has come an approach to grammar instruction, Processing Instruction (PI). PI as well as the research it has generated are described in Chapters 1 and 2 of this volume as well as in other publications (Benati, VanPatten & Wong 2005; Lee and VanPatten 2003; VanPatten 2003, 2004a).

At the heart of PI is the realisation that language instruction had been failing to address the issue of how learners process input. Instruction had focused on providing learners grammatical explanation followed by produc-

73

tion practices. VanPatten devised practices, called structured input practices, that first had learners processing the input without having to produce the target forms. As the research reviewed in Chapter 2 shows, PI improves the quality of the intake learners get and then supply to their developing systems. PI improves the form-meaning connections learners make and thus provides grammatically richer intake to the developing system. PI is, arguably, the current 'next big thing' in second language grammar instruction.

Another current 'next big thing' in language instruction in general is computer assisted language learning (CALL) or as we prefer, technology-enhanced language instruction. At one time debate surrounded the use of the computer for language learning and teaching. Presently, however, the focus of discussion is not on whether to accept technology, but on how to integrate it more effectively into the learning and teaching of languages (Liu, Moore, Graham and Lee 2003, p. 262). In VanPatten's 1996 monographic treatment of PI, he posed a question of a practical nature, 'Because PI is input-based, can computers deliver effective processing instruction?' (p. 158). We take up this question in this chapter as we empirically compare the results of delivering PI in classrooms, on computers, and in a hybridised environment combining elements of the classroom and the computer.

Review of literature

Our point of departure is PI itself. As described in Chapter 2, previous PI research has firmly established that PI is an effective approach to grammar instruction when compared directly to other types of instruction (Benati 2001; Cadierno 1995; Cheng 2004; Farley 2001; VanPatten and Cadierno 1993; VanPatten and Wong 2004). With this much evidence supporting the effectiveness of PI vis a vis other instruction, we decided to focus exclusively on PI and to manipulate other variables. We turned our attention to modes of delivering instruction. There are relatively few empirical investigations that compare the delivery of language instruction in computer and classroom environments and they address issues not relevant to the present study (Chang and Smith 1991; Sciarone and Meijer 1993).

Lee (2004) analysed the processing strategies that have been addressed in PI research. They include both syntactic and perceptual strategies. Learners misuse the syntax of Spanish Object-Verb-Subject sentences (Sanz 1997; VanPatten and Cadierno 1995; VanPatten and Fernández 2004; VanPatten and Oikennon 1996; VanPatten and Sanz 1995) and French causative sentences (VanPatten and Wong 2004); they misassign the grammatical of role of subject or agent to the first noun in the sentences. Learners do not perceive all the grammatical elements in the input. They have great difficulty perceiving these features in sentence medial position. Learners can, however, be taught via PI:

1) to process sentence medial verb morphology such as Spanish preterit (Cadierno 1995), Italian future tense (Benati 2001), and English simple past (Benati 2004b);

2) to perceive subjunctive verb forms in subordinate clauses (Chapter 5, this volume; Farley 2001, 2002, 2004); and

3) to process definite versus indefinite articles in French affirmative and negative sentences (Wong 2004b).

We extend this work to include two more linguistic items from Spanish: the preterite/imperfect distinction and negative informal commands. The preterite and imperfect are two past tenses in Spanish that convey aspect. The preterite is used for perfective aspect and the imperfect, as its name suggests, conveys imperfective aspect. Note the distinction at work in the following sentence.

> El teléfono sonó mientras Marta miraba la television.
> The phone rang while Marta was watching television.

Learners will have to learn to perceive the verbs endings in sentence internal positions and to use them to distinguish perfective and imperfective aspect. This study will address the Sentence Location Principle.

Spanish negative informal commands require a particular verbal morphology as well as the placement of a negative particle in preverbal position. The negative particle makes the verb morphology redundant and so learners will tend to ignore the verb morphology (VanPatten 2004b; Wong, 2004b). Wong (2004b) addressed the same processing problem, the Lexical Preference Principle, in her research on French affirmative/negative sentences and the definite versus indefinite article. PI will focus the learners on the verbal morphology of negative informal commands.

Research Questions

The present study is guided by the following research questions.

1. Are there differential effects for delivering Processing Instruction in different modes?

   a. textbook/classroom

   b. computer/ terminals

    c. individualised downloads of computer materials

2.   Are there differential effects for delivering Processing Instruction in different modes for different linguistic items?

    a. preterite/imperfect distinction

    b. negative informal commands

3.   Are there differential effects for delivering Processing Instruction in different modes for different linguistic items across time?

    a. pretest

    b. immediate posttest

    c. delayed posttest (1 week)

4.   Are there individual differences in the way some learners respond to Processing Instruction?

Research Design and Methodology

Participants

We solicited volunteer participants from Indiana University who were enrolled in nine intact classes (sections) of a first year Spanish course. All participants signed an informed consent and completed a background questionnaire. We used the questionnaire to screen subjects so that we included in the analyses only those who indicated that they were native speakers of English and that English was their home language. Three classes were randomly assigned to each of the three types of delivery: textbook, computer, or hybridised. All sections of the courses used the same textbook, *Viztazos: Un curso breve* 2nd (VanPatten, Lee, and Ballman, 2006); this book is based on the principles of Processing Instruction. All sections of the course utilised the same course syllabus, which was restricted so that the grammatical items we used in this study were not taught prior to treatment nor subsequent to our delayed posttest. We directed instructors of the classes not to review the treatment material after the treatment so that we could conduct a delayed posttest.

Table 4. 1 Timeline for the Study

Group →	Classroom	Computer	Individualised
Time ↓			
Week 1 Day 1	Informed consent Questionnaire Pretest: PID Pretest: NIC	Informed consent Questionnaire Pretest: PID Pretest: NIC	Informed consent Questionnaire Pretest: PID Pretest: NIC
Week 2	—	—	—
Week 3 Day 2	Treatment: PID Posttest 1: PID	Treatment: PID Posttest1: PID	Treatment: PID Posttest 1: PID
Week 4 Day 3	Posttest 2: PID Treatment: NIC Posttest 1: NIC	Posttest 2: PID Treatment: NIC Posttest 1: NIC	Posttest 2: PID Treatment: NIC Posttest 1: NIC
Week 5 Day 4	Posttest 2: NIC	Posttest 2: NIC	Posttest 2: NIC

PID = Preterite/imperfect distinction
NIC = Negative informal commands

We administered two pretests two weeks prior to the first treatment, one pretest per linguistic item. Following the procedure used in all previous PI research, we included in our analyses only those participants who scored less than 60% on both pretests. The mean pretest scores were 46% for preterite/imperfect distinction and 6% for negative informal commands. Additionally, to be included in the analyses, participants must have completed all elements of the study: 2 pretests, instruction on 2 linguistic items delivered in the same mode, 2 posttests, and 2 delayed posttests. From the first pretest to the delayed posttest for the second linguistic item, our study lasted five weeks although we were in classrooms or computer labs for only 4 days (see Table 4.1).

Given the rather stringent conditions used for participant screening as well as the student absences over a five week period, our attrition rate was quite high. Out of a potential pool of 192, we retained only 13% or 25 participants, 10 in the classroom mode, 8 in the computer mode, and 7 in the hybridised mode of delivering instruction. When reviewing these 25 participants' responses on the background questionnaire we discovered that 19 of these 25 had never studied any language other than Spanish but that 6 of the 25 had studied another language. These 6 subjects were native speakers of English and English was their home language. Spanish was not, however, the first foreign language they had studied. We carried out the statistical analyses using language study as a variable. We found no significant main effects (F $(1, 19)$ = .003; p = .958) and no significant interactions. Consequently, all 25 subjects remained in all statistical analyses and language study was removed as a variable from all statistical analyses because of the great imbalance in cell sizes (6 versus 19).

Materials

We based all our materials in the three modes of delivering PI on *Vistazos* (VanPatten, Lee, & Ballman, 2006). The textbook served as the set of materials for the classroom treatment group. From the textbook we created two other sets of materials for the other modes of delivering PI. As we describe the three sets of materials we underscore the extreme care we took to transpose the classroom textbook materials into the computer-delivered mode. Our goal was to offer learners the same type of instruction and practice distinguishable only by the mode of delivery. The materials for all three modes included two elements, explicit information about the linguistic item including processing information and structured input activities. We note that the explicit information provided learners is identical in all three modes because all learners received PI. We did not manipulate the type of instruction offered.

Classroom/Textbook

The layout and design features of the textbook are the same for both linguistic items we taught. Each linguistic item in the textbook is labelled 'Gramática esencial' [essential grammar] and provides learners with the forms they are to learn as well as an explanation of the forms and their functions. As set forward by PI proponents (e.g., VanPatten, 2004a; Wong, 2004a; Lee & VanPatten, 2003), explicit information should also draw learners' attention to the different processing problems they may face while dealing with any particular linguistic structure. Students are presented with a thorough explanation of the structure focusing on processing problems that students may have as part of this grammar point. After learners read the explicit information/explanation, they complete structured input activities (see Chapter 1 of this volume) that push learners to interpret the meaning of sentences by processing the target form. These activities are of different types that include matching sentences according to their meaning, communicative activities, reading, and comprehension activities. The explanation our learners received is provided in Appendix A. They can also be consulted in the original (VanPatten, Lee and Ballman, 2006, pp. 238–243 and pp. 253–255).

The explanations and practices in the textbook are accompanied by visuals such as pictures and photographs. Textual enhancements are also used to aid the learning process. The textbook also contains ancillary or complimentary material presented in boxes. This material gives more information about the topic under study, about aspects of the Spanish language or practical advice about learning Spanish. Another feature is called 'Los Hispanos hablan' [Hispanics speak], a videorecording of native speakers of Spanish from different countries commenting on the topic of the lesson. The features of the textbook are summarised in Table 4.2.

Table 4.2   Features of the Textbook

Characteristic	Type
Grammar	explicit information native language contrasts processing strategies
Visuals	pictures video information boxes
Textual enhancement	bold letters colours italicised letters different size letters
Activities	affective referential comprehension (listening and reading) communicative
Vocabulary	by topic translation different examples

The textbook also contains a bilingual vocabulary list at the end of each chapter and a bilingual end glossary. Because classroom learners can access these lists at any time, as well as ask the instructor for lexical support, we also included an online bilingual dictionary for the computer group and a printout of it for the hybridised group.

Computer materials

Our approach to developing instruction delivered on computers was informed by previous work in computer assisted language learning. In particular, Liu, Moore, Graham & Lee (2003) and Salaberry (2000) set forward suggestions of what needs to be addressed when planning studies in computer-based SLA. Liu et al. (2003) suggest that software needs to be based on relevant pedagogical and design principles for it to be effective. Similarly, Salaberry (2000) advocates that material designers need to assess critically both the features that characterise a potentially new type of literacy (i.e., the way learners interact with and respond to computers) and the effects of the computer's pedagogical capabilities. He also recommends that the assessment of the use of technology for language learning needs to be based on the analysis of how specific pedagogical objectives are achieved by means of the manipulation of specific characteristics of the technological tools. We took these factors into account.

We did not simply want to create exercises to be carried out on a computer. Because the textbook was created based on relevant and very solid pedagogical grounds, we set the goal to create a computer environment that truly mirrored what the authors of the textbook planned. Our goal was to create a computer *environment* just as the textbook materials, when delivered, are delivered in a classroom *environment*. To achieve our goal, we adapted the textbook materials described above to a computer environment using Macromedia Dreamweaver 6.0 and Flash 6.0 software. We were extraordinarily careful when manipulating the specific characteristics of the technology we were using so that any differences that might result across treatments would be due solely to the treatment, that is, solely to the mode of delivery.

We created a website for each of the two lessons and created a webpage with a navigation bar for each section of the lessons. The bar served to facilitate learners' navigation through the lesson. In this bar, we included a button for each of the activities that learners needed to complete during the class period. Learners accessed the different parts of the lesson by clicking the desired button. That is, while doing a structured input activity, they could also access the explicit information or the dictionary. In order to keep the classroom and computer environments parallel, we included the same textual enhancements and/or supplemental information charts in the computer environment that were in the textbook. We were careful not to include more enhancements or different enhancements than those presented in the textbook. We digitised all visuals from the book and embedded them in each webpage. Sample computer materials are provided in Appendix B.

Hybrid Mode Materials

Instructors present classroom materials to an audience of students resulting in instructor-to-student as well as student-to-student interactions. Individual students access computer materials and navigate themselves through a website completing the exercises as individuals not as members of a group and do so without an instructor. Classroom and computer modes of delivering instruction are obviously different from each other both as modes and for the format of the materials. We wanted to be certain that the format of the materials was not an extraneous variable and so we decided to create a third mode of delivering PI instruction. For the hybrid mode we downloaded the computer screens and created packets of materials for learners to complete individually (as was the case with the computer materials). We provided instructors with transparencies of the computer screens that they projected as they guided the class, working as individuals, through the materials. The instructor provided the audio for any activities that required it, as was the case with the classroom/textbook materials.

Table 4.3 summarises the characteristics and components of the materials we used and demonstrates the parallels between the three sets of materials.

Table 4.3 Caption

Characteristic	Type	Textbook	Computer Environment	Individualised Instruction
Grammar	Explicit information	√	Same	Same
	Native language	√	Same	Same
	Processing Strategies	√	Same	Same

Characteristic	Type	Textbook	Computer Environment	Individualised Instruction
Visuals	Pictures	√	Same	Same
	Video	√	Same	Same
	Information boxes	√	Same	Same
Textual Enhancement	Bold letters	√	Same	Same
	Colors	√	Same	Same
	Italicised letters	√	Same	Same
	Different size letters	√	Same	Same
Activities	Affective	√	Same	Same
	Referential	√	Same	Same
	Comprehension (Listening and Reading)	√	Same	Same
	Communicative	√	Same	Same
Vocabulary	By topic	√	Same	Same
	Translation	√	Same	Same
	Different examples	√	Same	Same

√ Characteristics present in the textbook
Same Characteristics same as that present on the textbook
Same Characteristics same as that present in the computer environment

Assessments

We designed two assessment tests, one per linguistic item. The tests are included in Appendix C. Near-native speakers and native speakers of Spanish reviewed the test items. We discarded any item that did not enjoy unanimous approval, meaning that only those test items that all reviewers agreed on were included. The preterite/imperfect distinction test was a multiple choice test divided into two sections: 5 unrelated sentences and a paragraph of 8 related sentences. The

5 unrelated sentences each contained two blanks so that there were 10 items in the unrelated sentence section and 11 items in the paragraph for a total possible score of 21. On all 21 items students selected either the preterite or imperfect form of the verb provided in parentheses.

The negative informal command test contained 5 scenarios presented in English. Each scenario requested that participants offer negative advice, such as 'don't buy beer for a person that suffers from alcoholism', by selecting the command from among four choices. This test contained a total of 14 multiple-choice options. In all 14 items, we used the present indicative, the preterite and the imperfect form of the verb as distracters. We created 3 different forms of each test by altering the order in which the items appeared. Each treatment group received a different form at each of the test administrations (see Table 4.4).

Table 4.4   Test Form administration

		Test Form		
		Pretest	**Posttest**	**Del. Post**
Mode	Computer	A	B	C
	Individualised	B	C	A
	Textbook	C	A	B

Results

Preliminary Determinations

Because the two assessment tests differed in the number of items they contained, we converted all scores to percentages and used percentages in our statistical analyses. We compared the mean scores on the pretests for each of the three treatment groups We first calculated an averaged score from the pretest scores on the two linguistic items. Their averaged pretest scores were quite similar: 27.0% for the classroom group, 27.3% for the computer group, and 27.2% for the hybrid group. We found no significant differences between the scores and will, therefore, attribute any differences we find in the posttest scores to the modes of delivering PI. As mentioned above, we detected a potentially extraneous intervening variable in that 6 of our 25 subjects had studied a language in addition to Spanish. We determined, however, that their scores were not significantly different from the scores of those who had only studied Spanish.

Table 4.5   Means and Standard Deviations for Pretest Scores

	PID	NIC	Grand Mean
Classroom N = 10	46.19% (8.41)	5.71% (5.63)	27.0%
Computer N = 8	46.43% (12.66)	6.25% (12.34)	27.3%
Hybrid N =7	46.26% (10.90)	6.12% (8.68)	27.2%

We performed a 3 X 2 X 3 repeated measures ANOVA using Mode as a between group factor and Linguistic Item and Time as within group factors. The descriptive statistics are given in Table 4.5 and 4.6. The statistical analyses yielded the following: no significant main effect for Mode of delivering PI $(F (2, 19) = .884; p = .429)$; no significant main effect for Linguistic Item $(F (1, 19) = .1.132; p = .301)$; but a significant main effect for Time $(F (2, 18) = 26.416; p = .0001)$. There were no significant interactions involving Mode but we did find a significant interaction between Linguistic Item and Time $(F (2, 18) = 15.498; p = .0001)$. To explore this interaction and the main effect for Time, we performed a series of paired means comparisons, specifically, a two-tailed t test. The results are presented in Table 4.7.

Table 4.6   Means (Standard Deviations) used in the 3 x 2 x 3 repeated measures ANOVA

	Time 1		Time 2		Time 3	
	PID	NIC	PID	NIC	PID	NIC
Classroom	46.19% (8.42)	5.71% (5.63)	60.00% (12.93)	67.85% (43.81)	60.00% (15.59)	68.57% (42.40)
Computer	46.43% (12.66)	6.25% (12.34)	56.55% (14.50)	81.25% (29.80)	64.29% (8.05)	77.68% (32.72)
Hybrid	46.26% (10.90)	6.12% (8.68)	51.02% ((16.66)	84.69% (25.23)	53.74% (23.28)	65.31% (37.67)

Table 4.7   Results of paired means comparisons (two-tailed t test)

Pair	df	t	p-value
Time 1 PID vs. NIC	24	17.094	.000*
Time 2 PID vs. NIC	24	-2.876	.008*
Time 3 PID vs. NIC	24	-1.446	.161
PID Time 1 vs. Time 2	24	-3.612	.001*
PID Time 2 vs. Time 3	24	-.851	.403
PID Time 1 vs. Time 3	24	-3.947	.001*
NIC Time 1 vs. Time 2	24	-8.958	.000*
NIC Time 2 vs. Time 3	24	2.031	.053
NIC Time 1 vs. Time 3	24	-7.636	.000*

PID = Preterite/imperfect distinction
NIC = Negative informal commands
* = $p < .05$ and the difference is statistically significant

The results of the t-tests revealed that the Time 1 (pretest) scores for preterite/imperfect distinction were significantly higher than those for negative informal commands. But at Time 2 (immediate posttest) the direction changes and the scores for negative informal commands are significantly higher than those for preterite/imperfect distinction. These two differences account for the interaction. The other comparisons revealed the nature of the main effect for Time. Learners benefited significantly from receiving Processing Instruction on both preterite/imperfect distinction and negative informal commands. We see this effect in that Time 2 scores are significantly higher than Time 1 scores. Learners retained the benefits of instruction (at least for a week). We see this effect in that Time 2 and Time 3 scores show no significant differences from each other and that Time 1 scores are significantly lower than Time 3 scores. PI is equally beneficial across three modes of delivering it and its effects are durative.

Individual Differences

One area that PI research has never explored is that of individual differences. Does PI affect some learners differently that it does others? To explore this question, we will examine our data qualitatively and quantitatively. In Table 4.8 we present different patterns of performance. From pretest to first posttest, Time 1 to Time 2, learners' scores could either improve, stay the same, or get worse. We took a change of 10% as the base rate. For example, if a learner's pretest score was 46% and his posttest score ranged from 37% to 55%, we classified him as no change in score. If his posttest score was 57% or above then we classified him as improved. If his posttest scores was 36% or lower, then we classified him as decreased score. Given the significant effect and interaction with the variable Time, we would expect that the vast majority of learners would have improved; and, they did. Improved performance, after receiving instruction, describes 64% of the learners on preterite/imperfect distinction and 88% of them with negative informal commands. Because we treated Linguistic Item as a within group variable, we can also determine how many of the learners improved on both linguistic items from pretest to posttest. That number is 6 or 24%, which we find surprisingly low. There were 9 learners who did not benefit from instruction on preterite/imperfect distinction; 6 of them showed no improvement in scores whereas 3 showed a decrease in score. Only 3 learners did not benefit from instruction on negative informal commands, and, these 3 showed a decrease in score from pretest to posttest. The zero in the column 'Both linguistic items' informs us that the 3 learners whose scores decreased on preterite/imperfect distinction were not the same 3 whose scores decreased on negative informal commands.

Table 4.8 Patterns of Performance per number of learners on each linguistic item

Pattern of Performance ↓	Preterite/imperfect Distinction	Negative informal commands	Both linguistic items
T1 to T2 Improved score (+10%)	16 = 64%	22 = 88%	6* = 24%
T1 to T2 No change in score (±9%)	6 = 24%	0	0

Pattern of Performance ↓	Preterite/imperfect Distinction	Negative informal commands	Both linguistic items
T1 to T2 Decreased score (-10%)	3 = 12%	3 = 12%	0
T2 to T3 Equivalent score (±9%)	9 = 36%	16 = 64%	6* = 24%
T2 to T3 Decreased score (-10%)	5 = 20%	6 = 24%	1 = 4%
T2 to T3 Improved score (+10%)	11 = 44%	3 = 12%	1 = 4%

*the same 6 people

From the immediate posttest to the delayed posttest, Time 2 to Time 3, learners' scores could have remained constant, decreased or improved. Given the results of the pairwise comparisons that showed no significant differences from Time 2 to Time 3 on either linguistic item, we would expect to find that the majority of learners had equivalent or improved scores. For preterite/imperfect distinction, 80% of learners' scores improved or remained constant. For negative informal commands, the number is 76%. On both linguistic items some learners' scores decreased from Time 2 to Time 3, 20% of learners for preterite/imperfect distinction and 24% for negative informal commands. Importantly, only one learner's scores decreased on both linguistic items. In essence, only one person in 25 did not derive a durative benefit of PI. PI is, then, good instruction.

Not one of the learners decreased their scores from Time 1 to Time 2 or from Time 2 to Time 3 on *both* linguistic items. This finding underscores the importance of our decision to include two different linguistic items. The interesting number among those describing performance from Time 2 to Time 3 is 6 or 24%. Six learners' scores on the preterite/imperfect distinction and on negative informal commands remained constant. These six learners are all the more remarkable in that they are the same six learners who improved from Time 1 to Time 2 on both linguistic items. In essence, what this qualitative analysis shows us is that only 6 of the 25 learners fit the pattern of the statistically significant differences! There are individual differences at work in the effects of PI on second language development.

We also analysed out data quantitatively in order to address individual differences. All previous PI research has used a score of less than 60% on the pretest as the criteria for including subjects in the data pool. We did the same in our study. The pretest scores on preterite/imperfect distinction averaged at 46% but they ranged from 27% to 57%. The pretest scores on negative informal commands averaged 7% but they ranged from 0% to 36%. We asked ourselves if there were subgroups within these ranges, and, we discovered that there were. Let's take the scores on the pretest for negative informal commands first. Thirteen of twenty five learners scored zero on the pretest; seven got one right, three two right. One scored three correct and another five correct of the fourteen items on the test. The range of scores on the pretest for negative informal commands is very limited.

We created three subgroups based on pretest scores. First, we address the PID data. We classified as High those learners whose pretest scores ranged from 50–59% (n = 11). We classified as Medium those whose pretest scores ranged from 40%-49% (n = 8). Finally, we classified as Low those who pretest scores were below 40%, i.e., 39%-24% (n = 6). We performed a one-way ANOVA and found a significant effect for Pretest Score ($F (2, 24) = 91.047$; $p = .0001$). The post hoc means comparisons revealed that the three groups were different from each other. Turning to the NIC data, we classified as High those learners whose pretest scores were 14% or higher (n = 5). We classified as Medium those whose scores were 7% (n = 7) and as Low those whose pretest scores were 0 (n = 13). We performed a one-way ANOVA and found a significant effect for Pretest Score ($F (2, 24) = 46.200$; $p = .0001$). The post hoc means comparison revealed that the three groups were different from each other.

What happens to these three different groups of learners once they receive instruction? Do the learners with greater knowledge at the outset have an advantage over the other learners? To address this question, we performed separate one-way ANOVAs for Time 2 and Time 3 using Pretest Score as the independent variable. For Preterite/imperfect distinction we found no significant effect for Pretest Score at Time 2 ($F (2, 24) = 1.245$; $p = .308$) nor at Time 3 ($F (2, 24) = .710$; $p = .710$). Post hoc means comparisons showed that there were no significant differences between any of the three groups at Times 2 and 3. The instruction these learners received levelled the differences between them. This result suggests that for PID, there may be a ceiling that none of the learners could exceed.

We performed the same analyses for the NIC data. With this data we did find significant effects for Pretest Score at Time 2 (F (2, 24) = 4.669; p = .020) and at Time 3 (F (2, 24) = 8.023; p = .002). The post hoc means comparisons showed a strange development. At Times 2 and 3, the mean scores of the groups of Medium and Low scorers were not significantly different from each other but they were significantly different from the mean scores of the High scoring group. They were significantly higher!

Because the differences between the groups changed after instruction, we decided to focus on each of the groups and determine how they performed over time. The general pattern of performance that we found was the Time 1 scores were significantly lower than Time 2 and Time 3 but that Time 2 and Time 3 scores were not significantly different from each other. Does this pattern of performance describe how High, Medium, and Low scoring learners responded to treatment? We performed a series of two-tailed t-tests to compare the means across time within each of the Pretest Score groups. We present the means and the results for PID in Table 4.9 and the means and results for NIC in Table 4.10.

Table 4.9   Mean scores for each group (hi, med, lo) for PID across time and the results of the paired samples T-Test

Pretest scores	N	Mean T1 (SD)	Mean T2 (SD)	Mean T3 (SD)	Effects
Hi	11	55.41% (2.40)	59.31% (16.82)	63.64% (10.71)	T1 = T2 T2 = T3 T1 < T3
Med	6	44.64% (2.47)	58.33% (12.66)	58.33% (16.21)	T1 < T2 T2 = T3 T1 = T3
Lo	8	31.75% (5.77)	48.41% (10.18)	53.97% (17.47)	T1 < T2 T2 = T3 T1 < T3

Table 4.8   Mean scores for each group (hi, med, lo) for NIC across time and the results of the paired samples T-Test

Pretest scores	N	Mean T1 (SD)	Mean T2 (SD)	Mean T3 (SD)	Effects
Hi	5	20.00% (9.31)	40.00% (45.34)	24.29% (17.93)	T1 = T2 T2 = T3 T1 = T3
Med	7	7.14% (0.00)	83.67% (24.99)	78.57% (35.23)	T1 < T2 T2 = T3 T1 < T3
Lo	13	0% (0)	87.36% (26.11)	84.07% (28.59)	T1 < T2 T2 = T3 T1 < T3

As seen in both tables, neither group of High scoring learners benefited significantly from instruction; there is no significant difference between their pretest and immediate posttest scores (T1 = T2). Both groups of Medium and Low scoring learners benefited significantly from instruction. Their immediate posttest scores are significantly higher than their pretest scores (T1 < T2). Instruction benefited those learners who needed it the most.

Finally, we would have liked to explore individual differences between groups based on Pretest Score and our main interest, Mode of Delivering Processing Instruction. We can not, however, do so because of the limited number of subjects per cell. As seen in Table 4.6, we have three cells with only 1 subject in them and 5 cells with only 2 subjects in them. We could not generalise any findings based on only 1 or 2 subjects.

Table 4.10 Subjects per cell for the Variables Pretest Score, Mode of Delivery, and Linguistic Item

Pretest Score	Classroom		Computer		Hydrib	
	PID	NIC	PID	NIC	PID	NIC
Hi	4	2	4	1	3	2
Med	3	4	2	2	3	1
Lo	3	4	2	5	1	4

Discussion and Conclusion

We return to our research questions in order to discuss our findings. First, we questioned whether there would be differential effects for delivering Processing Instruction in different modes. We very carefully transposed classroom materials into web-based materials in order to create a computer environment for delivering Processing Instruction. We then created a hybrid environment using features of a classroom plus the individualised computer materials. Our findings were very strong that there were no differences in learning outcomes across these three modes of delivering PI. The instruction is equally effective no matter how it is delivered. Our answer to VanPatten's question, '...can computers deliver effective processing instruction?' (1996, p. 158) is yes, they can. They do not, however, deliver it better than a person can do in a classroom.

Second, we questioned whether there would be differential effects for delivering PI in different modes for different linguistic items. To address this we selected linguistic items that presented different challenges to the learners. The aspectual distinction conveyed by Spanish preterite and imperfect past tenses is encoded morphologically at the end of the verb. The processing problem is that of the Sentence Location Principle. Our learners had already studied the forms and some uses of the preterite and separately had studied the forms and some of the uses of the imperfect. Our instruction on aspectual distinctions brought the two past tenses together as we taught learners to narrate in the past. Learners' mean pretest score of 46% indicated that they had some knowledge going into our treatments. We selected negative informal commands because they represented a new linguistic item, new forms and a new language function. The processing problem learners face is that of the Lexical Preference Principle. Learners' mean pretest score of 7% clearly underscores how novel this linguistic item was to the learners; 7% means that on average learners selected the correct negative informal command form only once out of the fourteen items on the pretest. We happily report that PI yielded significant improvement on both linguistic items. It is important to remember now that we treated the variable Linguistic Item as a within group variable, meaning that the same learners received PI on preterite/ imperfect distinction and on negative informal commands. We found that the same learners benefited greatly from PI on negative informal commands moving from 7% to 78% correct but less so on preterite/imperfect distinction moving from 46% to 56%. Because the learners are the same and the type of instruction is the same, the significant difference we found between the scores (78% versus 56%) must be due to the linguistic items themselves. In other words, PI can help students learn to narrate in the past, but learning aspectual distinction is difficult. It is more difficult to learn than it is to learn negative informal commands. We now add preterite/imperfect distinction and negative informal commands in Spanish to the list of linguistic items on which PI is effective instruction.

Additionally, we questioned whether we would find any effects for PI over time. We were able to conduct an immediate posttest and a delayed posttest one week later. Our results coincide with those of all previous research on PI that has included delayed posttesting. The effects of PI endure from a week to a month later (Benati 2004; Cadierno 1995; Farley 2001, 2004; VanPatten and Cadierno 1993; Wong 2004). We were unable to conduct any further delayed posttesting due to the fact that we conducted our research in regular classrooms. The week after we conducted the delayed posttest on negative informal commands, all our participants took the exam that included examining the two linguistic items we presented.

Finally, we explored individual differences. We found that only 6 of the 25 learners who participated in the study conformed to the pattern of performance described by the statistical findings. This finding showed us that some learners benefit more from PI than others and that some learners benefit from PI more on one linguistic item than they do on another. We also found that there might be a ceiling as to the effect of PI on learners' development with preterite/imperfect distinction. Whereas we could identify three groups of learners prior to instruction, we could only identify one group post-instruction. Learners' whose pretest scores we classified as Medium and Low benefited a great deal from PI whereas the High scoring learners did not benefit at all. The Medium and Low scoring learners came up to the level of the High scoring learners. We also found that High scoring learners on the NIC pretest did not benefit from instruction; they improved, but not significantly. The Medium and Low scoring learners benefited greatly from instruction. Their posttest scores far exceeded those of the High scoring learners and far exceeded scores on PID. Our take on the findings regarding individual differences is that for those who will benefit from instruction, they will benefit greatly from instruction (Stevick 1976).

Because our study examines instruction and its delivery, we will offer up certain, albeit restricted, pedagogical implications. Our findings do not indicate that computers will replace instructors any time soon. Computers are not better than instructors at delivering grammar instruction using a processing approach. Because we have found that PI can be delivered with equal benefit to students in either classroom or computer environments we see that some grammar instruction could be removed from the classroom and placed on the computer. The question then becomes What do you do with the class time that was once taken up by that grammar instruction? Our research provides no answer to this question but we recommend that class time be given over to activities that *require* face-to-face human interaction, preferably, task-based information exchange communicative activities (Lee 2000a; Lee and VanPatten 2003).

Conclusion

Our findings lead to the following conclusions.

1. Processing instruction can be delivered equally effectively in classroom and computer environments.

2. Processing instruction on different linguistic items can be taught equally effectively in classroom and computer environments.

3. The positive effects of Processing instruction on different linguistic items endures in classroom and computer environments.

4. Individual learners conform to the pattern of findings whereas other individuals do not.

5. Some individuals benefit more from PI than others.

Appendix A Explanation: Preterite/Imperfect Distinction

Narración en el pasado: Utilizando ambos el   y el imperfecto.

Pretérito   Imperfecto

Cuando mi mamá llamó,

yo meditaba. No hacía buen tiempo. Llovía y no quería salir de mi casa.

Ayer fui al gimnasio. Levanté pesas y luego corrí dos millas.

Mientras yo hacía ejercicio, mi compañera de cuarto trabajaba en el jardín.

As you know, there are two past tenses in Spanish: the preterite and the imperfect. Both tenses are needed and are used in combination when narrating events in the past because Spanish encodes what is called aspect

Aspect refers not to when an event happened, but to whether or not the event was in progress at the time referred to. As such, the use of the preterite and imperfect depends on how a narration unfolds and what relationship each event has to a time reference in the past.

Figure 4.1 Explanation: First computer screen for Preterite/Imperfect distinction

Narración en el pasado: Utilizando ambos el   y el imperfecto.

The preterite does not signal events in progress but it is used instead to refer to isolated events in the past, sequences of events, or to pinpoint a time in the past to which other events relate.   Isolated event in the past

Anoche me quedé en casa   Last night I stayed home.
Sequence of Events
Ayer jugué al tenis y luego me bañé en el jacuzzi.
Yesterday I played tennis and then I sat in the jacuzzi.
Pinpointing a time reference in the past

Cuando salí del cine ...   When I left the movie theater ...

Notice how in the following short narrative, the preterite and imperfect work together to show how the events relate to one another and to the time references included in the narrative.

First underline (make a list on a sheet of paper) the preterite forms and circle the imperfect forms you see. Then, for each use of the imperfect, see if you can tell at what point in time the event was in progress. The answers follow (cover the one ones in you book). Vamos!

Figure 4.2 Explanation: Second computer screen for Preterite/Imperfect distinction

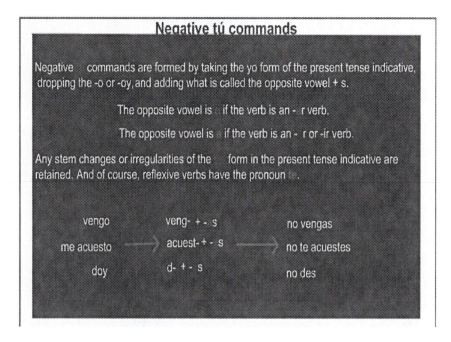

Figure 4.3 Explanation: Negative Informal Commands

Appendix B Sample Activity: Computer Environment, Preterite/Imperfect Distinction

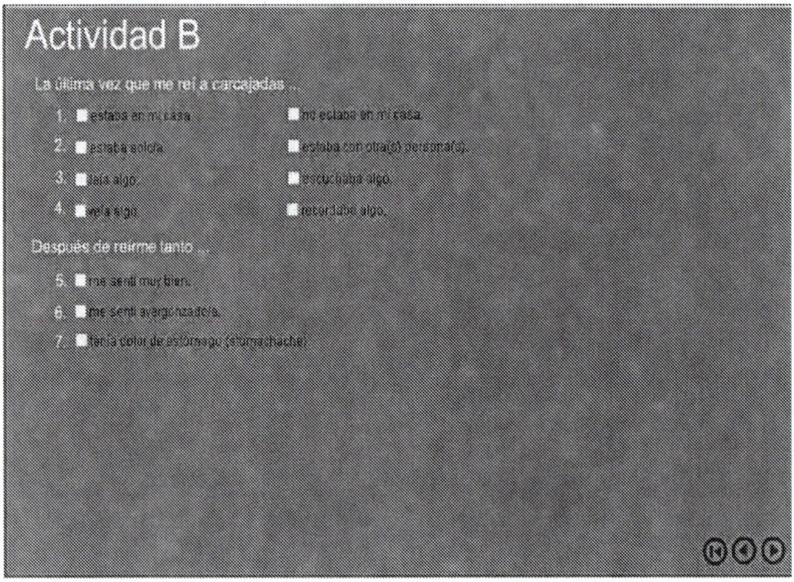

Figure 4.4 Sample Activity: Computer Environment, Preterite/Imperfect Distinction

Appendix C Assessment Task: Preterite/Imperfect Distinction

Pre-Test; Post-Test; Delayed Post-Test

Name _____ Section # _____ Code_____

A. To the best of your abilitiy, circle the appropriate response for each of the following sentences.

1. Yo _____ (mirar) la televisión cuand Pablo _____ (llamar) a la puerta.

    a. miré   a. llamó

    b. miraba   b. llamaba

2. Ayer, _____ (bañarse) y _____ (comer) antes de irme a clases.

    a. me bañaba   a. comí

    b. me bañé   b. comía

3. Anoche a las 7:00 _____ (llover) tanto que no _____ (poder) andar en bicicleta.

                  a. llovió   a. pude

                  b. llovía   b. podía

4. Mientras yo _____ (estudiar), Rosa _____ (hablar) por teléfono.

           a. estudié   a. habló

           b. estudiaba   b. hablaba

5. Cuando _____ (llegar) a la fiesta _____ (ser) las diez de la noche.

    a. llegaba   a. eran

    b. llegó   b. fueron

B. The following is a short passage about Pablo and his bad luck. To the best of your ability circle the appropriate response for each of the following sentences.

Ayer nuestro amigo Pablo **tenía/tuvo** muy mala suerte (luck). **Llegaba/Llegó** tarde a la clase de español. **Tuvo/tenía** mucho sueño porque la noche anterior **salía/salió** con unos amigos. En la clase mientras la profesora **explicó/explicaba** la lección, **Pablo se dormía/se durmió**. Luego **empezó/empezaba** a roncar (to snore). De repente sus compañeros lo **despertaban/despertaron**. La profesora **decía/dijo** furiosamente: "¡no te debes dormir en la clase! ¡Fuera de aquí!" Pablo **salía/salió** y **se marchaba/se marchó** a casa.

Assessment Task: Negative Informal Commands

Pre-Test; Post-test; Delayed Post-Test

Name: _____   Section # _____   Code _____

To the best of your ability, circle the appropriate response if you were recommending a friend not do something who was addicted to <u>alcohol</u> using the verb in parentheses.

1. comprar (to buy) cerveza
   a. No compres cerveza.
   b. No compraste cerveza.
   c. No compreas cerveza.
   d. No comprabas cerveza.

2. tomar (to have a drink) vino (wine)
   a. No tomas vino.
   b. No tomabas vino.
   c. No tomes vino.
   d. No tomaste vino.

To the best of your ability, circle the appropriate response if you were recommending a friend not do something who was addicted to <u>coffee</u> using the verb in parentheses.

3. ir (to go)
   a. No vas a Starbucks.
   b. No vayas a Starbucks.
   c. No ibas a Starbucks.
   d. No fuiste a Starbucks.

4. beber (to drink)
   a. No bebes café.
   b. No bebas café.
   c. No bebías café.
   d. No bebiste café.

To the best of your ability, circle the appropriate response if you were recommending a friend not do something who was addicted to <u>chocolate</u> using the verb in parentheses.

5. comer (to eat)
   a. No comas chocolate.
   b. No comes chocolate.
   c. No comías chocolate.
   d. No comiste chcolate.

6. preparar (to prepare, cook)
   a. No preparas un pastel de chocolate.
   b. No preparaste un pastel de chocolate.
   c. No preparabas un paste de chocolate.
   d. No prepares un pastel de chocolate.

Imagine that your cousin has won a contest to travel to Alaska in January. He or she wants some advice from you on what NOT to do while on his/her trip. To the best of your ability, circle the appropriate response if you were recommending your cousin <u>not</u> do something while in Alaska.

7. salir (to leave) abrigo (coat)
   a. No salías sin abrigo.
   b. No sales sin abrigo.
   c. No saliste sin abrigo.
   d. No salgas sin abrigo.

8. olvidar (to forget) guantes (gloves)
   a. No olvidaste tus guantes.
   b. No olvidess tus guantes.
   c. No olvidas tus guantes.
   d. No olvidabas tus guantes.

5   Comparing modes of delivering Processing Instruction and meaning-based output instruction on Italian and French subjunctive

Classroom research on the effects of formal instruction on second language acquisition (SLA) has principally focused on one main issue (Long 1983): whether grammar instruction per se makes a positive impact on second language acquisition. The question as to why and how we should teach grammar and particularly whether there is one type of grammar instruction which is more effective than others has been somewhat neglected. However, in the last few years we have witnessed an evolution in classroom research (Spada 1997, VanPatten 2004a, 2004b) investigating the effects of different forms of instructional intervention in SLA. This evolution is due partly to more studies having been carried out (Doughty & Williams 1998) that systematically describe how instruction is operationalised in the classroom, and, due in part to these studies having directly addressed the question of whether particular types of grammar instruction are more beneficial than others.

Within this research framework another relevant question arises regarding the role of grammar instruction. Is grammar instruction more effective when provided via one modality versus another (i.e., input vs. output)?

Van Patten (1996) has argued that a type of instruction, which he called PI, which helps learners to process information via input practice, might be more effective than that which requires learners to produce language too prematurely. PI is thought to be more effective than TI as it provides a more direct route for the learner to convert input to intake. The general findings of studies measuring the effects of PI (see Chapter two for a review of PI research) versus traditional output-based instruction, show that learners receiving PI always benefit in their ability to process input (interpretation tasks) as well as being able to access the target feature when performing production tasks.

Unlike TI where the focus of instruction is on the manipulation of the learners' output to effect changes in their developing system, PI aims to change the way input is perceived and processed by language learners. Unlike traditional output-based instruction which emphasised grammar rules and manipulative oral\written production practice, the purpose of PI is to alter how learners process input and to encourage better form-meaning mappings that result in a grammatically richer intake.

The role of input and output in SLA was and still is a point of contention among researchers and practitioners. Although, many studies and theories in SLA have provided evidence that input is the main ingredient and causative factor in SLA, further research is needed to determine what differential and complimentary possible effects input and output based instruction have on the acquisition of a variety of linguistic forms and structures. The purpose of the present study is to measure the possible effects of PI and MOI and to contrast different forms of delivering the two instructional treatments on the acquisition of Italian and French subjunctive, in particular, the subjunctive involving expressions of doubt, uncertainty, or disbelief. In the present study, PI consisted of explicit information (rule and psycholinguistic process) about the target feature followed by practice through structured input activities. MOI contained the same explicit information as in the case of the PI treatment followed by an output type of practice through structured output activities (Lee and VanPatten 1995, 2003). In addition to comparing the two instructional types, we also extended our research to include a comparison on classroom and computer modes for delivering the two instruction types. Is instruction more or equally effective delivered in different modes? Is there an interaction between instruction type and delivery mode? Is there an interaction between assessment (interpretation and production) and delivery mode?

Background

Research evidence contrasting PI and TI

PI has been contrasted to TI in a number of studies that could be defined as conceptual replications of the first study conducted by VanPatten and Cadierno (1993). This study, which is also referred to as 'the original study,' investigated the effects of PI on the acquisition of word order and object pronouns in Spanish with the aim of altering a default strategy used by L2 learners who assign the role of agent to the first noun they encounter in a sentence. This strategy is also known as 'The First Noun Strategy' and is incorporated into VanPatten's model as (P2) The First Noun Principle. For example, learners would misinterpret a sentence such as *La visita el chico* as 'She visits the boy' rather than the correct meaning of the sentence 'The boy visits her' [her-visits-the boy].

VanPatten and Cadierno addressed two main questions:

1. Does altering the way in which learners process input have an effect on their developing system?;

2. If there is an effect, would that effect be observable in both learners' processing as well as in learners' output?

Van Patten & Cadierno (1993) compared three groups of students of Spanish at intermediate level who received two different instructional 'treatments' (2 hours instruction on two consecutive days). One group received a very 'traditional' type of instruction based on a widely adopted college-level text-book that emphasised grammar explanation and oral-written production. The second group received PI. And, a third group served as a control group and received no instruction. A total of eighty second year students learning Spanish at university level participated in this study in which a pre-test\post-test design was used to measure the possible effects of instruction. VanPatten and Cadierno developed two different assessment tasks. The first was an interpretation task in which learners heard ten sentences along with five distracters. Five of these sentences were of the order, object pronoun-verb-subject and the other five were of the order object marker +noun-object pronoun-verb-subject. The five distracters were simply subject-verb-object sentences. The groups, after hearing a sentence, had just a few seconds to select one of the drawings projected on an overhead screen in front of the class.

The other assessment task was a sentence-level written production task in which the three groups were given five items to complete. Each item consisted of a two-part sentence that corresponded to a two-part drawing. The second part of the sentence was incomplete and the student's task was to complete it based on the visual cues.

Van Patten and Cadierno (1993) showed that PI is very beneficial for learners. First of all, this approach to grammar instruction improved learners' ability to interpret object pronouns in Spanish correctly. Furthermore the results demonstrated the positive effects of PI on learners' production. PI effects were not limited to input processing but were also observable in output. We once again underscore that in PI research, the PI group never produces the target features through output practice. The positive effects of PI on interpretation and production tasks would be found over and over again (see Chapter 2).

To investigate the effects of PI on a different processing problem Cadierno (1995) investigated the effects of PI on the acquisition of a morphological linguistic item of Spanish. She researched the impact of PI on the acquisition of Spanish *preterite tense*. Cadierno's study focussed on the lexical preference processing strategy: 'learners process lexical items as opposed to grammatical form when both encode the same semantic information' (Van Patten 1996:97).

The aim of PI was to push learners to attend to elements in the input that might be otherwise missed. She taught learners to process the grammatical forms and to encourage them to do so, she stripped the input of lexical markers for past tense. Spanish 'preterite tense' is very difficult morphologically for L2 learners; there are 16 different forms for the regular 'preterite tense' owing to the inflections for both tense and person-number and the type of verb being inflected. The design of Cadierno's study is identical to the previous one in terms of: proficiency level of the subject pool used for the experiment (intermediate), type of treatment (PI vs. TI), assessment tasks (interpretation & production written task) and procedures for data collection (pre-test and post-test).

Sixty intermediate Spanish learners at university level were involved in this study. The PI group was, as expected, significantly superior to the other two groups (TI and control) on the interpretation task. The results also showed that the PI group who never engaged in production type activities during instruction, performed as well as the TI group in the sentence level written production task. The results were durative up to a month later. Overall these results give support to the key role of input processing in SLA.

The 'traditional' group managed to perform the production task but were not able to perform in the interpretation task. TI seemed to have very little effect on interpretation. According to Van Patten & Cadierno (1993: 238) a possible explanation is that the TI group 'learned to perform the task and did not acquire any new language'. Another possibility, which is more tenable, is that grammar explanation and practice 'do not enhance how learners process input and therefore do not provide intake for the developing system'.

With the intention of generalising the findings from the first two studies and address some of their limitations, many other studies have been conducted in various languages on various linguistic features (Buck 2000 on the acquisition of the present continuous in English, Cheng 1995 on Spanish copular verbs (*ser* and *estar*), VanPatten & Wong 2004 on the French *faire* causative). The results from these studies clearly indicated that the previous findings from VanPatten and Cadierno (1993) could be generalised to different linguistic items and different processing problems (Lee 2004).

VanPatten and Cadierno designed the PI and TI treatments to be different from each other. The explicit information they gave PI learners was different from the explicit information they gave TI learners. The SIA for PI required learners to search for meaning and connect it to form. The output practices for TI were drill-oriented (mechanical, meaningful and communicative drills). Were the structured input activities too meaning focussed? Were the output practices too mechanical?

Benati (2001) designed a study on the acquisition of Italian morphology (future tense) comparing PI vs. TI. As was the case with Cadierno (1995), Benati sought to alter the 'Lexical Processing Strategy' (P1 .b) as well as to address a methodological concern about the meaningfulness of TI activities. Second semester undergraduate university students (the final pool consisted of 39 participants) were the subjects of this study. Two experimental groups received PI and TI, respectively. A third group served as a control group and although they received no instruction on the target feature they received a comparable amount of exposure to the target feature. Benati prepared two different packs of materials and provided instruction over a period of two days (6 hours). Subjects took pre-tests on interpretation and production before the beginning of the instructional treatment and post-tests immediately after the end of the instructional treatment and a follow-up set battery after three weeks. Three tests were produced, one for the interpretation task and two for the production task: a written completion task and an oral limited response task.

In this study Benati balanced very carefully the use of mechanical and form-oriented activities with the use of more meaningful activities in the TI treatment. The results of this study were similar but not identical to Cadierno's (1995). Both PI and TI groups improve significantly on the production tests. The statistical analysis revealed that the PI group performed better than the TI group and the control group on the interpretation task but that the TI group's performance improved from the pre to the posttest when compared to the performance of the control group. Benati (2001) argued that the difference might have been due to the types of activities used in the TI treatment; it contained a balance of mechanical and communicative practices. By creating meaningful output, subjects might have created language that served as input to others. The issue is whether one learner's output can serve as another's input.

Research evidence contrasting PI and MOI

Farley (2001a) compared the effects of PI vs. MOI on the acquisition of the Spanish subjunctive of doubt. He selected the subjunctive because it occurs in dependent clauses and presents learners the problems captured in the Sentence Location and Meaning-Before-Non Meaning Principles. Learners tend to process items in sentence initial position before those in final position and those in medial position. In Spanish the subjunctive is located in medial position where it is least likely to be processed. In the sentence *No creo que entienda el problema* (I do not believe he/she understands the problem) the subjunctive inflection (the – *a*- of *entienda*) is in the middle of the sentence and the Sentence Location Principle predicts that learners will overlook the subjunctive inflection because it is not located in a more salient position. The Spanish subjunctive also is redundant and not very meaningful. The matrix clause provides the semantic information and triggers the verb form of the dependent clause.

The final pool in this experiment consisted of fifty university students studying Spanish at intermediate level. The material for the PI treatment was developed following the guidelines for structured input activities (e.g. VanPatten and Sanz 1995; Lee and VanPatten 1995, 2003; Farley, 2005). Unlike TI, the MOI contained no mechanical drills and the activities developed for the treatment were based on the tenets of structured-output activities proposed in Lee and VanPatten (1995). Unlike TI, the MOI and PI groups received the same processing-oriented explicit information. Both the PI and the MOI groups were exposed to two days of instruction and assessed following a pre-test/post-test design that included interpretation and production tasks.

Farley's results differed from the previous studies comparing PI vs. TI. Both the PI and MOI groups made equal and significant improvements on both the interpretation and the production tests. Farley attributed the equal performance of the two treatments to one main factor. The MOI treatment is different from TI as it does not contain mechanical drills practice and its communicative and interactive nature might have resulted in incidental input. He argued (Farley, 2001a) that the MOI treatment used in his study was not a pure output treatment as the MOI 'is not an instruction type that is entirely input free; when learners responded during the follow-up phase of each activity their utterances served as incidental input for their classmates: the incidentally focused input made the subjunctive more salient than it would be with raw, unfocused input' (p.76). He considered that the incidental input learners received during output practice and not output practice itself was responsible for learners' performance. It must be also noticed that in an identical study (same structure, design and procedure) conducted by Farley (2001a) the results showed that although the PI and MOI groups made similar gains from a pre-test to a post-test, the PI gains were maintained in a delayed post-test whereas the effects of the MOI treatment declined. Morgan-Short and Bowden (2006) also show declining effects for MOI.

Benati (2005) conducted an experiment investigating the effects of PI, TI and MOI on the acquisition of English simple past tense. The subjects were Chinese (47 subjects) and Greek (30 subjects) school-age learners of English residing in their respective countries. The participants in both schools were divided into three groups. The first group received PI, the second group TI, and the third group MOI. Benati used one interpretation and one production task in a pretest/posttest design (immediate effects only). The results showed that PI had positive effects on the processing and acquisition of the target feature. In this study the PI group performed better than the TI and MOI groups on the interpretation task and the three groups made equal gains on the production task. The PI treatment was superior to the TI and MOI treatment in terms of helping learners to interpret utterances containing the English simple past. PI successfully taught learners to process forms in the input rather than to rely on lexical items to signal past. The results of the statistical analysis indicated that PI, TI and MOI made an equal improvement (from pre-test to post-test) on the production task (sentence-level task). These findings on production mirror those in previous studies. PI not only has an impact on the way learners interpret sentences but also on the way learners produce sentences. PI has clearly altered the way learners processed input and this had an effect on their developing system and subsequently on what the subjects could access for production.

Gely (2005) compared the effects of PI and MOI on the acquisition of French imperfect tense (Lexical Preference Principle). Fifty-two college students were enrolled in second year French. However, only thirty-three constituted the final pool. One group received PI, the second group MOI, and the third group acted as a control group. The latter received no instruction. Gely developed three different tasks: an interpretation task and two production tasks (completion text and a written production task). The outcomes of this study showed what we have come to expect. The PI group outperformed the other two on the interpretation task and that the PI and MOI groups were equal on the production tasks. Gely confirmed they results in delayed posttest given three weeks later.

Interestingly, the results from Benati's (2005) and Gely's studies (2005) differ from Farley's (Farley, 2001a and 2001b). Both studies provide evidence indicating that PI is better than output oriented instruction no matter whether output instruction is mechanical (as previous research comparing PI vs. TI has clearly showed) or meaning based practice. This finding held for a different linguistic feature (English Past Simple Tense) in different languages (English and French), and on different L1's (Greek and Chinese school-age learners). Benati (2005) and Gely (2005) confirm the consistency and effectiveness of PI in improving learners' performance in both interpretation and production tasks. Subjects receiving MOI did not also develop the ability to interpret utterances correctly.

Motivation for the present study

The results of the studies briefly reviewed in the previous section have demonstrated that when PI is compared to TI or a type of TI in which the amount of meaning-based activities is increased we obtain generally superior effects for PI. However, when we have compared PI to MOI we have obtained conflicting results.

On the one hand, Farley (Farley's 2001a, and 2001b) showed that MOI could have an equal effect to PI on interpretation and production tasks. On the other hand, Benati (2005) and Gely (2005) yielded overall superior effects for PI. The question is: why did the PI and MOI groups in Farley's (Farley's 2001a, and 2001b) studies perform similarly and why do these studies differ from the other two studies (Benati 2005, Gely 2005)? Would the nature of the MOI treatment be the explanation for the conflicting results? Would the particular structure (subjunctive) investigated in Farley's studies (Farley's 2001a, and 2001b) cause the results to be different than the other studies contrasting MOI and PI?

It remains to be determined whether the subjunctive (a morphological form that depends on the semantics of the matrix clause) is the reason we find effects for MOI on the interpretation tasks. Clearly, it is important to examine further the acquisition of the subjunctive. Additionally, we can contribute more information to this question if we also examine the effects of PI and MOI through different modes of delivery (classroom versus computer). Do we obtain similar or different results if we contrast the effects of PI to MOI delivered via computer terminal. Identifying the causative variables for the positive effects of MOI would also have pedagogical implications in developing a foreign language teaching curricula that combines the beneficial components of both PI and MOI in a single technologically enhanced instruction type.

Research Questions

The aim of the present study is to compare and contrast two instructional treatments (PI and MOI) and at the same time to measure the effects of two different modes of delivering the same instructional treatments on the acquisition of Italian subjunctive of doubt and opinion and French subjunctive of doubt. We formulated two specific questions:

1:    What are the relative effects of PI and MOI in two different modes of delivery (via classroom instruction vs. computer terminals) on the acquisition of Italian Subjunctive of Doubt and Opinion and French Subjunctive of Doubt as measured on a sentence level interpretation task?

2: What are the relative effects of PI and MOI in two different modes of delivery (via classroom instruction vs. computer terminals) on the acquisition of Italian Subjunctive of Doubt and Opinion and French Subjunctive of Doubt as measured on a sentence level written production task?

Design

Participants and Procedure

We carried out two separate experimental classroom studies (see overview of the experiment in Table 5.1) in order to investigate the relative effects of PI and MOI delivered through two different modes in the acquisition of Italian and French subjunctive of doubt and opinion.

In the first experiment (Italian subjunctive of doubt and opinion) participants were enrolled in a second semester undergraduate intermediate course in Italian as part of their language degree in a British university. In the final data pool English native speaker students (all female, aged 20–21) were distributed randomly to the four groups (PI-classroom, PI-computer, MOI-classroom, MOI-computer).

We reduced the original sample of subjects (64) to 47 subjects (final data pool). We removed any subject who might have had some previous experience in the target language or who could practice the target language outside class. Additionally, we excluded participants who scored more than 60% on the pretest. The reduced sample consisted of PI classroom group ($n = 9$), MOI classroom group ($n = 10$), PI computer group ($n = 14$), and MOI computer group ($n = 14$).

In the second experiment (French subjunctive of doubt) all the subjects were enrolled in a second semester undergraduate beginner course in French that they were studying as part of their language degree in a British university. We began with 80 subjects but then only sixty one participants took part in the final experiment; they were all aged 20–21 with half male and half female. We assigned subjects to treatment groups randomly. We removed subjects from the final data pool if they had contact with French outside of class and if they scored over 60% on the pretest. As a result of these measures we formed four groups: PI classroom group ($n = 17$), MOI classroom group ($n = 15$), PI computer group ($n = 16$), and MOI computer group ($n = 13$).

We purposefully designed the two experiments to be parallel and therefore comparable. Initially we had planned to match the groups in both experiments across various characteristics (GCSE results, sex, age, and so forth) in order to increase cross-study comparability. We found, however, that the number of variables for successfully matching two small groups was impossible and so, we randomised group membership instead by drawing names out of a box. Randomisation of sample groups obviates the need to consider individual variation (Skehan, 1989) and is the most effective way to assure group comparability. Randomisation minimises the influence that extraneous variables, such as motivation, aptitude, intelligence, might have on test scores. We assume then that the effects of any extraneous variables will affect the different groups in the same way.

We screened subjects in both experiments based on certain responses to a background questionnaire. For subjects to be included in the data pool: their native language had to be English; their target language learning had to be limited to classroom instruction; and, they must not have had previous experience or linguistic knowledge of the target language. Additionally, only those learners who had participated in all phases of the treatment were included in the final data analyses. The independent variables in both studies were instructional treatment (PI vs. MOI) and mode of delivery (classroom vs. computer). Instruction took place across two consecutive days (two hours per day) of instruction and practice on the target feature. We balanced the instructional materials in every way except for the type of practice the students received (i.e. input vs. output practice) and the mode of delivery (instructor in the classroom vs. computer).

Table 5.1   Overview of the experiment

RANDOMISATION
PRE_TEST (Interpretation & Production)

INSTRUCTIONAL TREATMENTS
    PI
    PI comp
    MOI
    MOI comp

2 CONSECUTIVE DAYS
4 HOURS

POST-TESTS (Interpretation & Production)

The regular classroom instructor taught the two groups that received classroom instruction. In the classroom, he acted as a facilitator during the experiment. This instructor asked the other group of students to perform the activities on computer terminals.

Target grammar feature: Italian subjunctive

We selected the subjunctive as our target for a number of reasons. Firstly, because of the processing principle (The Sentence Location Principle) investigated in this study. According to VanPatten (2002, 2004b) learners tend to process items in a sentence that are located in initial position before those in final position and those in medial position. This processing strategy has been investigated in previous studies (Farley, 2001a, 2001b, 2004). In Italian the subjunctive is located in the medial position where it is least likely to be processed. In the sentence *Non penso che parli bene italiano* (I do not believe he/she speaks Italian well) the subjunctive inflection (the – *i* of *parli*) is in the middle of the sentence and the Sentence Location Principle predicts that learners will overlook the subjunctive inflection because it is not located in a more salient position.

Secondly another principle that might effect the processing of the acquisition of the Italian subjunctive in nominal clauses after expressions of doubt is the 'Lexical Preference Principle'. This processing strategy has been investigated in many PI studies (e.g. Cadierno, 1995; Benati, 2001). VanPatten (2004b) states that learners will tend to rely on lexical items as opposed to grammatical form to get meaning when both encode the same semantic information. In a sentence like *Non penso che canti bene* (I doubt that he/she sings) the nonaffirmative phrase 'non penso' expresses doubt to the learner. Learners would have no need to attend to the subjunctive verb ending (-*i* in *canti*) because it simply re-communicates the non-affirmation already expressed by the lexical items in the main clause.

Thirdly, many argue that the matrix clause of subjunctive sentences carry meaning whereas the verb form in the dependent clause is simply triggered. As a triggered verb form it carries no semantic meaning. The subjunctive verb form in the dependent clause can also be seen as a redundant nonmeaningful form. Learners face two more processing problems captured by the The Preference for Nonredundancy Principle and The Meaning-Before-Non Meaning Principle.

Target feature: French Subjunctive

The French subjunctive is also a complicated linguistic feature to acquire as it appears in complex structures of the language (e.g. nominal and adverbial and adjectival clauses). For the purpose of this study the use of the present subjunctive after expression of doubt was investigated. The use of the subjunctive to express doubt in French is very similar to other Romance languages. It does occur in expression of doubt such as *Je doute que* (I doubt that) or *Je ne crois pas que* (I do not believe that). As in the case of the Italian subjunctive, the French subjunctive of doubt is affected by the same processing problems described above. In the sentence *Je doute qu'il vienne* (I doubt that he comes) learners would attend the word *doute* to encode the sentence as expressing the idea of doubt. They do not need to pay attention to the subjunctive form *vienne* of the nominal subordinate clause to get the meaning of the sentence (P1 .b). The other processing problem learners face is that of the verb's location in the sentence. In the sentence *Je doute qu'il vienne* (I doubt that he comes) the subjunctive form *vienne* is in final position and in the sentence *Je doute qu'elle prenne de vacances* (I doubt she takes some holidays) the subjunctive form *prenne* is in medial position. The forms are not in preferred processing positions.

Instructional treatments

We used two instructional treatments in both experiments. The first group, received the PI treatment via classroom instruction; the second group received the same PI treatment but via a computer terminal; the third was exposed to the MOI treatment via classroom instruction; the fourth group received the MOI treatment via computer terminal. We developed two sets of instructional materials in which we balanced all the activities in terms of activity types and visuals. We provided the exact same vocabulary (which consisted in highly frequent items) across the treatments. We provided an equal amount of practice with the target form in both sets of instructional materials.

The four groups received the exact same explicit information prior to practice regarding the target feature so that the only difference between the treatments was limited to the nature of the practice and the mode of delivery. (See Appendix A for the Italian subjunctive and Appendix B for the French subjunctive.) We frist developed the classroom materials and from those developed the computer materials. The guidelines proposed by Lee and VanPatten (1995, 2003) served as the basis for developing the instructional materials for both PI and MOI. We produced ten activities for each instructional treatment consisting of ten practice items for each activity.

The technical point of view

As stated, we started with the paper-based activities and adapted them for computer delivery. The students were able to complete the activities in exactly the same way as they would if completing the exercises with pen and paper. The technology used to create these exercises was Macromedia Flash and Action Script programming language. Macromedia Flash is a fairly new technology that allows for much more interactivity and animation than standard web pages and it is also very well suited for developing on-line activities.

Altogether we converted 10 paper activities (for each treatment) for the Italian subjunctive and the French subjunctive into an online format. First we created a design for the interface; this was a simple yet neat design that would be consistent in all exercises. Most activities involved listening to a sound file, conjugating a verb by filling in a blank or ticking a box to give an opinion about a statement. Here we added certain features to give the exercises a real time effect. These included only allowing the students to hear audio files once in referential structured input activities. In affective structured input activities the computer would total up the number of wrong and rights or positive and negative opinions and at the end give conclusions based on these totals. The computer activities had the functionality of paper-based activities.

PI (two different modes of delivery)

The packet of material used for the PI treatment contained explicit information (including information about the processing principle) and structured input activities. We provide sample activities in Appendix C for the Italian subjunctive and Appendix D for the French subjunctive. An equal number of referential and affective activities were developed. The material for both the traditional paper based language activities and the activities developed for computer delivery were the same and were developed on the basis of the guidelines principles for the construction of structured input activities presented in Lee and VanPatten (1995, 2003) and VanPatten and Sanz (1995). In the PI treatment, all the activities were developed in order to address the processing problems described in the previous section. The main clause was separated from the subordinate clause to take advantage of primacy effects that cause a form in an initial position to be processed more easily than a form in a medial position. In the referential activities because the subordinate clause was separated from the matrix clause, participants were not able to rely on the lexical item (subjunctive triggers) to determine that doubt was expressed. Participants in this group were forced to attend to the subjunctive or indicative forms to determine whether or not doubt or opinion was expressed by selecting the corresponding trigger. As PI aims to force learners to process form to get meaning (in this case the subjunctive), no activities were developed where learners had to produce the targeted grammatical item. The activities in this instructional treatment were all communicative and meaningful and were constructed in an attempt to alter the processing problem addressed in this study. Only one grammatical form was presented in both the Italian (third person subjunctives in nominal clauses after expression of doubt and opinion) and the French subjunctive (third person subjunctives in nominal clauses after expression of doubt). Participants had to read or listen (they were only allowed to hear the sentence once) to the input through the computer activities or via classroom instruction (depending on the mode of delivery of the two treatments) and had to make decisions about what they read or heard.

In referential activities, participants were required to select the correct trigger (matrix clause) or subordinate clause to complete each sentence. Implicit feedback was provided by the computer or by the instructor responding "OK" or "correct" if the user's response was correct. "Wrong" displayed on the screen if participants had chosen an incorrect response. Learners were told whether they were right or wrong but no explanation as to why was given. This procedure is in keeping with the purpose of structured input activities which is to push learners to a different processing strategy. This can only happen if the participants receive information that an interpretation is incorrect.

MOI (two different modes of delivery)

The treatment consisted of grammatical explanation (same as the PI groups) and meaning-based output practice. We provide sample activities in Appendix C for the Italian subjunctive and Appendix D for the French subjunctive). As in the case of the PI treatment, the material for both the traditional paper based language activities and the activities developed for computer delivery were the same. No mechanical activities were included in the output practice. The structured output activities used in the MOI treatment in the present study were developed following the guidelines provided by Lee and VanPatten

(1995, 2003). Students were required to produce the linguistic feature and were always engaged in communicatively-oriented output practice. As Lee and VanPatten (1995: 121) state, structured output activities have two main characteristics: 1) 'They involve the exchange of previously unknown information'; and 2) 'They require learners to access a particular form or structure in order to express meaning'. The focus was on one form and one meaning (using subjunctive in sentences expressing doubt or opinion) and participants in the MOI treatment had to respond to the content of the output. We provide sample activities in Appendix C for the Italian subjunctive and Appendix D for the French subjunctive.

Assessment

We used a pre-test/post-test design in both classroom experiments. See Figure 5.1. We administered the pre-tests two weeks before the beginning of the instructional period. The pre-test was also used to eliminate subjects from the original pool. Anyone who scored 60% or better on either of the two assessment measures was not included in the final pool. The tests, which we piloted, were balanced in terms of difficulty and vocabulary (high frequency items). See Appendix E for the Italian and Appendix F for French tests. We designed two versions of the tests, one interpretation task and one written production task, in order to form a split block design. The PI groups received version A as the pre-test, while the MOI groups received version B. In the post-test, the PI groups received version B and the MOI groups version A. The interpretation task consisted of 20 sentences (10 distracters item in the Present Tense expressing certainty) of which 10 were in the Subjunctive (expressing doubt or opinion).

The participants had to listen to the dependent clause of the sentences and indicate (interpret) whether the independent clause would express doubt or certainty. No repetition was provided so that the test would measure real-time comprehension. In the interpretation task the raw scores were calculated as follows: incorrect response = 0 points, correct response = 1 point. The written production task was developed and used to measure learner's ability to produce correct sentences using the subjunctive. The students were required to transform 10 sentences in the subjunctive form. The same scoring procedure was used in this discrete item test (correct form = 1 point; incorrect form = 0 points). The production task was not a spontaneous task and allowed learners to monitor their responses and to provide their answers in writing.

Results

Interpretation task (Italian subjunctive)

We performed an ANOVA on the pre-test scores for the first experiment; they showed no significant differences among the instructional treatment means before instruction ($F(3,47) = 3.324, p = .28$). We will attribute any differences we find in their posttest scores to the effects of our treatments. We used a repeated measures ANOVA to compare the effects of Treatment and Time on the interpretation task. The statistical analysis yielded very interesting results. It revealed a significant main effect for Treatment ($F(3,47) = 37.702, p = .000$) and for Time $F(3,47) = 19.257, p = .000$), as well as a significant interaction between Treatment and Time ($F(3,47) =.740, p = .000$). The descriptive analysis in Table 5.2 clearly indicates that the two PI groups significantly improved from pre-test to post-test. The MOI classroom group minimally improved and the MOI computer group did not improve.

We performed a *post-hoc* Tukey test on the raw scores to determine possible differences between the four treatment groups. It revealed the following contrasts: the scores of the PI classroom group and PI computer group were not significantly different ($p = .995$); the PI classroom group's scores were significantly better than both the MOI classroom group's ($p= .002$) and the MOI computer group's ($p = .000$); the PI computer group's scores were also significantly better than both the MOI classroom group's ($p = .000$) and the MOI computer group's scores ($p = .000$); the MOI classroom group's scores were better than MOI computer group's (p = .006). The results are presented graphically in Graph 5.1.

Table 5.2   Means and standard deviation (Italian data) for Interpretation task pre-test and post-test

Variable	n	Pre-test		Post-test 1	
		Mean	SD	Mean	SD
PI comp	14	2.3571	.63332	8.1429	1.09945
MOI comp	14	3.1429	.66299	3.6429	.49725
PI class	9	2.5556	.88192	8.0000	1.50000
MOI class	10	2.3000	.94868	5.6000	1.83787

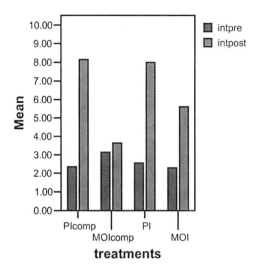

Figure 5.1 Means by instructional treatment for interpretation task (pretest and posttest for Italian subjunctive

Written production task (Italian subjunctive)

The ANOVA carried out on the pre-test scores showed no statistically significant difference between the groups (F 3, 47) = 2.323, p = .088) before the beginning of the instructional period. We then performed a repeated measures ANOVA on the raw scores of the pretest/post-test written production task in order to compare the effects of Treatment and Time. The statistical analysis revealed no effect for treatment ($F(3,47)$ = .185, p = .906) and no interaction between Treatment and Time($F(3,47)$ = .770, p = .517). It did, however, show a significant effect for Time $F(3,47)$ = .505, p = .000). The means in Table 5.3 showed that the four groups improved almost equally from the pre to the post-test.

We performed a *post-hoc* Tukey test on the raw scores to determine which differences accounted for the effect for Time. The results revealed that all the groups improved their performance from pretest to posttest and that each group had made equal gains from the pre-test to the post-test. Results are graphically shown in Graph 5.2.

Table 5.3   Means and standard deviation (Italian data) for Production task pre-test and post-test

		Pre-test		Post-test 1	
Variable	n	Mean	SD	Mean	SD
PI comp	14	2.2143	.80178	7.7857	1.62569
MOI comp	14	2.1429	.86444	7.5000	1.40055
PI class	9	1.5556	.88192	7.8889	1.61589
MOI class	10	1.7000	.67495	7.5170	1.50923

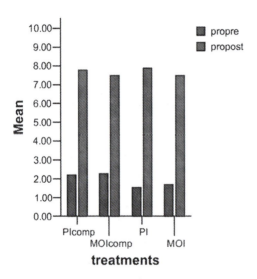

Figure 5.2   Means by instructional treatment for production task (pretest and posttest for Italian subjunctive

Interpretation task (French subjunctive)

Our procedures for analysing the French data are the same as for the Italian data. We conducted an ANOVA comparing the pre-test scores on the interpretation test. We found no significant differences among the four groups in the different instructional treatments before instruction ($F(3,61) = .238$ $p = .870$). We will attribute any differences in posttest scores to our treatments. We used a repeated measures ANOVA to compare the effects of Treatment and Time on the results of the interpretation task. The statistical analysis provided very similar results to the previous experiment with Italian data. It revealed significant main effects for Treatment ($F(3,61) = 375.810, p = .000$), and for Time $F(3,61) = 59.355$, $p = .000$) as well as a significant interaction between Treatment and Time ($F(3,61) =.51.169, p = .000$).

The means in Table 5.4 show that the two PI groups improved from pre-test to post-test. The MOI classroom group minimally improved whereas the MOI computer group did not improve. We carried out a *post-hoc* Tukey test to determine possible differences in the four groups. It revealed the following contrasts: the PI classroom group's and PI computer group's scores were not significantly different ($p = .878$); the PI classroom group's score was significantly better than both the MOI classroom group's ($p= .000$) and the MOI computer group's scores ($p = .000$); the PI computer group's score was also significantly better than both MOI classroom group's ($p = .000$) and the MOI computer group's scores ($p = .000$). The MOI classroom group's score was not, however, significantly better than MOI computer group's ($p = .279$). The results are displayed in Graph 5.3.

Table 5.4 Means and standard deviation (French data) for Interpretation task pre-test and post-test

Variable	N	Pre-test		Post-test 1	
		Mean	SD	Mean	SD
PI comp	16	1.31	.946	7.19	1.905
MOI comp	13	1.08	.954	1.69	.751
PI class	17	1.12	.857	7.82	1.380
MOI class	15	1.07	.961	2.87	.640

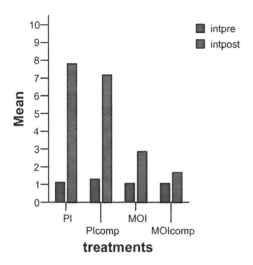

Figure 5.3 Means by instructional treatment for interpretation task (pretest and posttest for French subjunctive

Production task (French subjunctive)

We used an ANOVA to compare scores on pre-test for the production task. The analysis revealed no significant difference between the groups (F 3, 61) = 2.501, p = .068) before instruction. We then performed a repeated measures ANOVA using on the raw scores on the pretest/post-test written production task. This statistical analysis was used to compare the effects of Treatment and Time. The analysis showed no effect for Treatment (F(3,61) = 1.508, p = .222) nor an interaction between Treatment and Time F(3,61) = 2.501, p = .168). It did, however, show a significant effect for Time F(3,61) = 770.275, p = .000).

The means in Table 5.5 show that the four groups improved almost equally from the pre to the post-test. A *post-hoc* Tukey test confirmed that the posttest scores of the four groups were not significantly different from each other. All groups improved on the production task and improved equally. The results are graphically shown in Graph 5.4.

Table 5.5 Means and standard deviation (French data) for Production task pre-test and post-test

| Variable | N | Pre-test | | Post-test 1 | |
		Mean	SD	Mean	SD
PI comp	16	1.00	1.003	5.94	1.611

MOI comp	13	1.38	.870	6.54	1.506
PI class	17	.59	.618	6.35	.786
MOI class	15	.73	.779	6.67	1.345

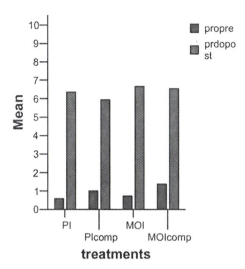

Figure 5.4 Means by instructional treatment for production task (pretest and posttest for French subjunctive

Summary of Results

The first question of this study was formulated to investigate the effects of PI, and MOI on the interpretation of sentences containing the targeted feature (subjunctive of opinion and doubt in Italian and subjunctive of doubt in French) in two different modes of delivery. The results of the statistical analysis (see summary of ANOVA in Table 5.6) for both the Italian and French experiments clearly showed that the PI treatment made significant improvement (from pre-test to post-test) on the interpretation task.

Table 5.6   Summary of Repeated Measures ANOVA

Data	df	SS	MS	F	p
Italian inter					
Treatment	3	177.097	59.032	37.702	.000 *
Time	3	66.489	22.163	19.257	.000 *
Time x Treatment	3	3.584	1.195	740	.000 *
Italian prod					
Treatment	3	1.307	436	185	.906
Time	3	2.187	729	505	.000 *
Time x Treatment	3	3.584	1.195	770	.517
French inter					
Treatment	3	424.456	143.456	375.810	.000 *
Time	3	201.114	67.038	59.355	.000 *
Time x Treatment	3	221.040	73.680	51.619	.000 *
French prod					
Treatment	3	5.263	1.754	1.508	.222
Time	3	896.100	784.100	770.375	.000 *
Time x Treatment	3	5.282	1.761	2.501	.168

The PI treatment delivered via classroom instruction and computer terminals was superior than the MOI treatment delivered via the same modes, in terms of helping learners to interpret utterances containing the subjunctive that expresses doubt and opinion (see summary of the post-hoc analysis in Table 5.7). Despite the mode of delivery PI is a successful intervention in altering learners processing strategies and instilling new ones (in this case the 'Sentence Location Principle' and the 'Lexical Preference Principle'). In the case of the Italian data the MOI treatment delivered via classroom instruction was better than the MOI treatment delivered via computer terminals.

The second question of this study sought to investigate the effects of PI and MOI through two different modes of delivery on producing sentences containing the Italian and French subjunctive expressing doubt and opinion. The results of the statistical analysis indicated that PI and MOI groups made equal improvement (from pre-test to post-test) on the production task. The groups were equal and the different modes of delivery made no difference. The evidence obtained in the study on the production task suggests that the effects of PI not only have an impact on the way learners interpret sentences but also on the way learners produce sentences.

Table 5.7 Summary of post-hoc analysis

Italian data inter- pretation	Italian data production	French data interpretation	Italian data production
PI class = PI group	PI class = PI comp =	PI class = PI group	PI class = PI comp
PI class > MOI class	MOI class = MOI	PI class > MOI class	= MOI class = MOI
PI class > MOI comp	comp	PI class > MOI comp	comp
PI comp > MOI class		PI comp > MOI class	
PI comp > MOI comp		PI comp > MOI comp	
MOI class > MOI comp		MOI class = MOI comp	

Discussion and Conclusion

The overall findings from the present study support the results obtained by the majority of studies investigating the effects of PI, which show that PI is superior to output based instruction. In addition this study provides further empirical support for the view that PI is better than MOI (Benati, 2005; Gely, 2005). The results of the present study differ from Farley's research (Farley, 2001a, 2001b) as it indicates that PI is better than MOI in helping learners to process the subjunctive of doubt in French and subjunctive of doubt and opinion in Italian. Therefore, despite the difficulty for English native speakers to process the targeted linguistic feature (as argued by Farley, 2004) PI is a better form of intervention than MOI.

The results obtained in the two parallel studies confirm the effective- ness of PI in improving learners' performance in both interpretation and production tasks. Learners exposed to the MOI treatment did not make any improvement from the pre-test to the post-test on the interpretation task. However, in the case of the Italian data the MOI group who received the treatment through classroom instruction performed better than the MOI group who received the same treatment but via computer terminals. This was not the case for the data collected in French. In the interpretation task learners receiving MOI via the two different modes of delivery did not make any substantial improvement from the pre and post-test and their performance was not statistically significant.

A possible explanation for the results obtained in these parallel studies and particularly the results obtained in the Italian data could be the fact that both treatments were compared through different modes of delivery. In the case of the MOI and PI treatments delivered via computer terminals, learners did not receive input from an instructor or from interacting with other learners. The fact that in the case of the MOI treatment delivered via computer terminals, participants received no incidental structured input, unlike in the case of Farley's studies (Farley, 2001a, 2001b), seems to explain the results obtained in these parallel studies.

The MOI treatment delivered through two different modes and containing meaning based activities was not successful at producing positive effects (altering the processing problem) on students' performance. As argued by Lee and VanPatten, while output practice 'may help with fluency and accuracy in production, it is not "responsible" for getting the grammar into the learners' head' (1995: 95).

The results from the studies presented in this paper have made a number of contributions to the ongoing debate on the effects of PI when contrasted to MOI.

First of all the outcomes from these parallel studies have confirmed the positive role of PI as an instructional intervention designed to alter processing problems and consequently to have an impact on learners' developing systems. The results from the present study clearly indicate that no matter how PI is delivered it is a successful instructional treatment as it helps learners to make form-meaning connections for acquisition.

Secondly, the outcomes from these studies have shown that the MOI treatment, despite the way it is delivered, is not successful in bringing about similar effects to those brought about by PI. The better performance in the interpretation task in the Italian data obtained by the MOI classroom group in contrast with the other MOI computer group could be explained in terms of the form of delivering instruction and practice. In the case of MOI treatment delivered via classroom instruction participants might have been affected by incidental structured input. MOI activities were meaningful activities that encouraged learners to express opinions and doubts. It is plausible that participants' responses and answers in the MOI activities might have served as incidental structured input for the other subjects in the group (Farley 2004b).

Thirdly, the fact that in the two different modes of delivery the PI groups performed better than the MOI groups in the interpretation task in both studies clearly indicated that structured input activities are the causative factor in the improved performance of learners as all groups received the same amount and type of explicit information and the only difference was practice (structured input activities vs. structured output activities).

Structured input activities are the main component and the causative variable for the change in performance (see summary of the results investigating the effects of PI and its components in VanPatten, 2002; Benati, 2004a, 2004b; and Chapter 2). It seems obvious to us that the most effective instruction would put input practice before output practice.

The findings from the present study have shown that PI not only has an impact on learners' ability to process input better but also has an impact on their developing system so that they can access a linguistic feature in written production tasks under controlled situations. However, the nature of the production task used in this study might lead itself to the use of conscious knowledge. A production test that includes time pressure and does not allow students to monitor their responses might have been produced different results altogether. It is necessary to contrast the effects of PI vs. MOI or other output-based techniques through both discourse level interpretation and production tasks as in the present study only sentence-level tasks were used.

The results from these parallel experiments clearly indicate that PI is an effective way to incorporate focus on form into a communicative framework and can be delivered effectively in different modes. Perhaps we can maximise the amount of time subjects spend practicing grammar through structure input activities by including PI as part of participants coursework or making better use of the computer to deliver PI.

Appendix A

EXPLICT INFORMATION

<u>The Italian Subjunctive of doubt and opinion</u>

Subjunctive expresses uncertainty, doubt rather than fact. It also conveys the opinion and attitudes of the speaker.

The subjunctive verb is located either at the end of the sentence (e.g. Io non credo che parli) or in the middle of the sentence (e.g Io non credo che parli bene il francese).

The subjunctive is generally preceded by a main clause (independent) and the conjunction *che.*

ATTENZIONE

When the verb or expression in the independent clause denotes certainty, the present indicative is used in the dependent clause.

When the verb or expression in the independent clause expresses opinion, doubt or uncertainty, the present subjunctive is used

Compare these pairs of sentences :

So che Paolo non parla inglese Penso che Parlo non parli inglese
Sono certo che Giorgio canta Dubito che Giorgio canti

Expressions indicating opinion, doubt

Credo
Dubito
Ho l'impressione
Immagino
Penso

Expressions indicating certainty

So
Sono sicuro
Sono certo
Sono convinto

The present subjunctive is formed by adding the appropriate ending (third person singular) to the verb stem.

Lavor-i
Scriv-a
Dorm-a

Appendix B

EXPLICIT INFORMATION

The French subjunctive of doubt.

Subjunctive expresses uncertainty, doubt rather than fact.

The subjunctive verb is located either at the end of the sentence (e.g. Je ne suis pas sûr qu'il veuille) or in the middle of the senntence (e.g Je ne crois pas qu'il prenne des vacances).

The subjunctive expresses the idea of doubt already expressed in the first part of the sentence.

ATTENTION

When the verb or expression in the independent clause denotes opinion or certainty, the present indicative is used in the dependent clause.

When the verb or expression in the independent clause expresses doubt or uncertainty, the present subjunctive is used in the dependent clause.

Compare these sentences:

Je pense qu'il vient
Je ne crois pas qu'il prenne des vacances

Expressions indicating doubt

Je ne crois pas
Je ne pense pas

Expressions indicating certainty

Je suis sûr
Je suis persuadé

Appendix C

(see on-line activities produced for this study in the following web site: http://www.wilburontheweb.co.uk/langproject/)

Processing Instruction

Attività 1 : « Conoscete il vostro professore ? »

You will here the second half of a sentence concerning your teacher. First, tick the appropriate opinion phrase to fit each statement, then say if you agree or not which each statement.

		D'accordo	Non D'accordo
1	❑ a. Non penso che … ❑ b. Sono certo che…	❑	❑
2	❑ a. Dubito che… ❑ b. So che…	❑	❑
3	❑ a. Sono sicuro che… ❑ b. Non Penso che…	❑	❑

		D'accordo	Non D'accordo
<u>4</u>	❑ a. Temo che… ❑ b. Sono certo che…	❑	❑
<u>5</u>	❑ a. Non credo che… ❑ b. So che…	❑	❑
<u>6</u>	❑ a. Non sono sicuro che… ❑ b. Sono certo che…	❑	❑
<u>7</u>	❑ a. Sono sicuro che… ❑ b. Non Penso che…	❑	❑
<u>8</u>	❑ a. Non penso che… ❑ b. Sono certo che…	❑	❑
<u>9</u>	❑ a. Non credo che… ❑ b. So che…	❑	❑
<u>10</u>	❑ a. Dubito che… ❑ b. Sono certo che…	❑	❑

Sentence heard by learner:

1. *sia sposato*
2. *ha una vespa*
3. *sia ricco*
4. *non ha un cane*
5. *tifi perla Juventus*
6. *ha due figli*
7. *sappia cantare*
8. *sia un bravo insegnante*
9. *gioca a Tennis*
10 *conosce bene l'Inglese.*

Attività 2 : « Il Principe Carlo »

Answer the following questions by ticking the 'si' or 'no' box.

Non Penso che il Pricipe Carlo....

	Si	No
1	❏	❏
2	❏	❏
3	❏	❏
4	❏	❏
6	❏	❏
5	❏	❏
6	❏	❏
7	❏	❏
8	❏	❏
9	❏	❏
10	❏	❏

Sentence heard by learner:

1. *debba sposarsi ?*
2. *sia un buon reale ?*
3. *sia una brava persona ?*
4. *sia un buon padre ?*
5. *abbia molte qualità umane ?*
6. *sia simpatico ?*
7. *sia bello ?*

8. *faccia delle cose buone ?*
9. *sia fotogenico ?*
10. *possa essere il nuovo re ?*

Meaning output-based instruction

Attività 1 : « George Bush, politico ideale ? »

Complete the following sentences by putting the verb in bracket at the correct tense and answer the question at the bottom.

1. **Non credo che Bush...**   a. _____ (essere) un politico intelligente.

   b. _____ (conoscere) le lingue straniere.

   c. _____ (avere) buon senso.

   d. _____ (rispettare) l'ambiente

   e. _____ (diventare) il prossimo presidente .

2. **Sono certo che Bush...**   a. _____ (essere) disonesto.

   b. _____ (essere) un bugiardo.

   c. _____ (giocare) a tennis.

   d. _____ (essere) sposato

   e. _____ (amare) il suo paese

Non Pensi che Bush sia il politico ideale? Perchè ?_____

Attività 2 : « Conoscete il vostro professore ? »

You will hear the first half of a sentence that somebody made concerning your teacher. First, complete the sentence with the verb in brackets in the appropriate tense according to the prompt you hear, then say if you agree or not which each statement by ticking the appropriate box.

		Si	No
1	_____ (bere) molto whisky.	❏	❏
2	_____ (essere) sposato.	❏	❏
3	_____ (giocare) a tennis.	❏	❏

		Si	No
4	_____ (tifare) per la Juventus.	❏	❏
5	_____ (essere) un buon insegnante.	❏	❏
6	_____ (avere) una vespa.	❏	❏
7	_____ (parlare) bene l'inglese.	❏	❏
8	_____ (sapere) cucinare.	❏	❏
9	_____ (avere) un cane.	❏	❏
10	_____ (fare) arti marziali.	❏	❏

Sentence heard by learner:

1. *Non credo che…*
2. *Sono certo che…*
3. *So che…*
4. *Non penso che…*
5. *So che…*
6. *Sono sicuro che…*
7. *So che…*
8. *Non credo che…*
9. *Non penso che…*
10 *Dubito che…*

Appendix D

(see on-line activities produced for this study in the following web site:

http://www.wilburontheweb.co.uk/langproject/)

Processing Instruction

Activité 1 : « Martin : le mari ideal ? »

A friend of you describes Martin but you only hear the second half of each of his statement. Find out what he said by ticking the appropriate opinion phrase to fit each statement.

	Je doute que Martin...	Je sais qu'il...	
1	☐	☐	soit riche.
2	☐	☐	finisse tôt le travail.
3	☐	☐	sort beaucoup le soir.
4	☐	☐	vient souvent chez ses parents.
5	☐	☐	veuille des enfants.

In your opinion, would Martin be a good husband ?
☐ oui   ☐ non

Activité 2: « Britney Spears »

Here are some opinions about Britney Spears. Say if you agree or disagree with these opinions by ticking the appropriate box.

Je ne crois pas que Britney Spears...

	D'accord	Pas d'accord
1	☐	☐
2	☐	☐
3	☐	☐
4	☐	☐

	D'accord	Pas d'accord
5	❑	❑
6	❑	❑
7	❑	❑

Sentence heard by learner:

1. *soit très intelligente.*
2. *ait un style original.*
3. *fasse de la bonne musique.*
4. *vende beaucoup de disques en France.*
5. *prenne de la drogue.*
6. *dise des choses intéressantes.*
7. *plaise à beaucoup de monde.*

Meaning output-based instruction

Activité 1 : « Martin : Le mari idéal ? »

Complete the following sentences by putting the verb in bracket at the correct tense and answer the question at the bottom.

1. **Je ne crois pas que Martin...**
   a. _____ (être) riche.
   b. _____ (finir) tôt le travail.
   c. _____ (vouloir) des enfants.

2. **Je sais que Martin...**
   a. _____ (sortir) beaucoup le soir.
   b. _____ (venir) souvent chez ses parents.

Est-ce que Martin est le mari idéal ? Pourquoi ? _____

Activité 2 : « Britney Spears »

Complete the prompts in the table with the items given to you according to your opinion on Britney Spears. Remember to make the appropriate tense changes.

a. être très intelligente.
b. avoir un style original.
c. faire de la bonne musique.
d. vendre beaucoup de disques en France.
e. prendre de la drogue.
f. dire des choses intéressantes.
g. plaire à beaucoup de monde.

	Je crois que **Britney Spears...**	**Je ne crois pas que** **Britney Spears...**
1		
2		
3		
4		
5		
6		
7		

Appendix E

INTERPRETATION TEST

You will hear the end of 20 sentences. Tick the appropriate beginning for each sentence you hear in the table below.

1	❑	Dubito che	❑	So che
2	❑	Non penso che	❑	Sono certo che
3	❑	Credo che	❑	Sono certo che
4	❑	Penso che	❑	Sono convinto che
5	❑	Non sono sicuro che	❑	Sono certo che
6	❑	Dubito che	❑	Sono certo che
7	❑	Penso che	❑	So che

8	❏	Dubito che	❏	So che
9	❏	Non penso che	❏	Sono certo che
10	❏	Non Credo che	❏	Sono certo che
11	❏	Penso che	❏	Sono convinto che
12	❏	Non sono sicuro che	❏	Sono certo che
13	❏	Dubito che	❏	Sono certo che
14	❏	Immagino che	❏	So che
15	❏	Dubito che	❏	So che
16	❏	Ho l'impressione che	❏	Sono certo che
17	❏	Credo che	❏	Sono certo che
18	❏	Penso che	❏	Sono convinto che
19	❏	Non sono sicuro che	❏	Sono certo che
20	❏	Immagino che	❏	Sono certo che

PRODUCTION TEST

Complete the following sentences by putting the verb in brackets at the appropriate tense.

1   Non penso che l'italiano _____ (essere) facile.

2   Penso che Paolo_____ (avere) abbastanza soldi.

3   Immagino che Alessandro_____ (parlare) molte lingue.

4   Credo che Giorgio_____ (giocare) bene a tennis.

5   Ho l'impressione che lui _____ (amare) molto l'Italia.

6   Dubito che lei _____ (scrivere) bene.

7   Non sono convinto che Giovanna _____ (viaggiare) molto per il mondo.

8   Non sono sicuro che Paola _____ (guidare) la macchina bene.

9   Penso che Marco _____ (lavorare) tutto il giorno.

10 Non credo che Anna _____ (dormire) fino a tardi la mattina.

Appendix F

INTERPRETATION TEST

You will hear the end of 20 sentences. Tick the appropriate beginning for each sentence you hear in the table below.

1	❑ Je doute qu'il ❑ Je sais qu'il	11 ❑ Je sais qu'elle ❑ Je ne crois pas qu'elle
2	❑ Je ne pense pas qu'elle ❑ Je suis persuadée qu'elle	12 ❑ Je ne crois pas que mon chien ❑ Je pense que mon chien
3	❑ Je doute qu'il ❑ Je crois qu'il	13 ❑ Je ne crois pas qu'il ❑ Je pense qu'il
4	❑ Je pense qu'elle ❑ Je ne suis pas sûr qu'elle	14 ❑ Je sais qu'il ❑ Je doute qu'il
5	❑ Je crois qu'elle ❑ Je doute qu'elle	15 ❑ Je pense qu'elle ❑ Je ne pense pas qu'elle
6	❑ Je sais qu'elle ❑ Je ne crois pas qu'elle	16 ❑ Je doute qu'elle ❑ Je sais qu'elle
7	❑ Je pense qu'il ❑ Je ne crois pas qu'il	17 ❑ Je crois qu'elle ❑ Je doute qu'elle
8	❑ Je ne pense pas qu'il ❑ Je crois qu'il	18 ❑ Je ne crois pas qu'il ❑ Je pense qu'il
9	❑ Je pense qu'il ❑ Je ne crois pas qu'il	19 ❑ Je crois qu'il ❑ Je ne pense pas qu'il
10	❑ Je crois qu'il ❑ Je doute qu'il	20 ❑ Je suis sûr qu'elle ❑ Je ne suis pas certain qu'elle

PRODUCTION TEST

Complete the following sentences by putting the verb in brackets at the appropriate tense.

1   Je ne pense pas que le français _____ (être) facile.

2   Je pense qu'elle _____ (suivre) des cours de danse.

3   Je pense qu'il _____ (vouloir) se remarier.

4   Je doute que Marie _____ (prendre) l'avion seule.

5   Je ne suis pas sûr qu'il _____ (avoir) envie d'aller au cinéma.

6   Je sais que Paul _____ (venir) souvent à la maison.

7   Je ne suis pas certain qu'elle me _____ (rejoindre) en Italie.

8   Je ne crois pas qu'elle _____ (conduire) bien.

9   Je pense que Jean _____ (réussir) bien dans son travail.

10   Je ne crois pas qu'il _____ (savoir) jouer du piano.

11   Je sais qu'il _____ (faire) bien la cuisine.

12   Je doute que mon professeur _____ (boire) beaucoup de vin.

13   Je crois que son fils _____ (vivre) en Afrique.

14   Je doute qu'il _____ (aller) en Espagne cet été.

15   Je ne crois pas que mon père _____ (vouloir) voyager aux Etats-Unis.

16   Je sais que la ville _____ (construire) une nouvelle université.

17   Je crois que Marc _____ (lire) beaucoup la presse.

18   Je pense qu'il _____ (dormir) trop.

19   Je ne suis pas sûr qu'Hélène _____ (dire) la vérité.

20   Je suis sûr qu'elle _____ (pouvoir) faire ça pour toi.

6   Summary, conclusions, and recommendations for the practice of PI

In this, the final chapter of the volume we will summarise the findings of the new empirical research we presented in Chapters 3–5, and place it in the context of previous research on PI. We will then extrapolate the pedagogical implications of our research, focusing not only on delivering PI in classrooms and on computers, but on PI as part of a sequence of learning activities for grammar instruction that move learners from processing input to producing output.

Our findings in the larger research context

Processing problems and principles

The research presented in Chapter 3 on the effects of PI on learning Japanese past tense forms and affirmative versus negative present tense forms addressed two processing problems. Japanese past tense forms are verb-final morphological inflections (-*mashita*) that easily co-occur with lexical adverbials (e.g., *kaisha* 'yesterday'). Learners tend to prefer using the adverbial to establish a temporal reference over using the verb inflection. We hypothesise that this preference would be made stronger by the fact the canonical word order in Japanese places the verb in sentence final position. The verbal inflection for tense would be the last linguistic element in the sentence. Learners would have 'to wait' till the end of the sentence to process the temporal framework.

Japanese present tense is encoded via a verb-final morphological inflection, one for affirmative (-*su*) and another for negative (-*sen*) denotations. Our instruction was not focused on tense assignment but rather on whether the sentence was affirmative or negative. In this case, the processing problem we addressed was the location of the grammatical/semantic information: word-final and sentence-final position.

Spanish preterit/imperfect aspectual distinction (Chapter 4) is encoded as a verb-final morphological inflection (e.g., *visitó* [preterit] versus *visitaba* [imperfect]). Spanish word order, while flexible, would tend to place verbs in sentence medial position. Based on the sentence location principle, neither sentence medial nor verb-final position is a favoured processing position. Additionally, many lexical adverbials convey aspectual distinction such as *el verano pasado* 'last summer' versus *todos los veranos* 'every summer'. Processing instruction on aspectual distinction in Spanish would also have to address the lexical preference and sentence location principles.

Spanish negative informal commands (Chapter 4) are formed with a preverbally placed lexical negator and with a verb-final morphological inflection. Once learners encounter the preverbal negator the verb morphology, although meaningful, becomes redundant and so instruction on negative informal commands would have to address the preference for non-redundancy principle.

Italian and French subjunctive mood to express doubt (Chapter 5) occur in complex sentences constituted by independent and dependent clauses. The expression of doubt occurs in the independent clause and is expressed lexically. This expression of doubt triggers the subjunctive verb form in the dependent clause. The subjunctive form of the verb is encoded as a verb-final morphological inflection. The lexical trigger makes the subjunctive morphology redundant and is, therefore, less likely to be processed. We can not strip the input of the lexical trigger as we do when teaching tense and aspect because the trigger is obligatory. Rather, we must manipulate the input so that learners process the subjunctive form first in order to pair it with the appropriate trigger.

We have updated Table 2.1 from Chapter 2 to now include the research we presented in this volume. Table 6.1 presents an overview of the linguistic items used to investigate various of VanPatten's Processing Principles (VanPatten 2004b).

Table 6.1   Revised overview of the processing problems addressed in PI research

Processing Principle Van Patten 2004b	Linguistic Items Investigated	Study
P2. The First Noun Principle. Learners tend to process the first noun or pronoun they encounter in a sentence as the subject/ agent	1. Spanish object pronouns	1. Sanz 1997, 2004; VanPatten & Cadierno 1993; VanPatten & Fernández 2004; VanPatten & Oikennon 1996; VanPatten & Sanz 1995
	2. French causative	2. VanPatten & Wong 2004

Processing Principle Van Patten 2004b	Linguistic Items Investigated	Study
P1b. The Lexical Preference Principle. Learners will tend to rely on lexical items as opposed to grammatical form to get meaning when both encode the same semantic information	1. Spanish preterite tense 2. Italian future tense 3. Spanish subjunctive 4. English simple past tense 5. French negation and indefinite articles 6. Japanese past tense 7. Spanish preterite/ imperfect distinction 8. Italian subjunctive 9. French subjunctive	1. Cadierno 1995 2. Benati 2001, 2004a 3. Farley 2001, 2004 4. Benati 2005 5. Wong 2004 6. Lee & Benati 2007 7. Lee & Benati with Aguilar-Sánchez & McNulty 2007 8. Lee & Benati 2007 9. Lee & Benati 2007
P1c. The Preference for Non-redundancy Principle. Learners are more likely to process nonredundant meaningful grammatical form before they process redundant meaningful forms. P1d. The Meaning-Before-Nonmeaning Principle. Learners are more likely to process meaningful grammatical forms before nonmeaningful forms irrespective of redundancy.	1. Italian gender agreement with adjectives 2. Spanish subjunctive 3. French negation and indefinite articles 4. Spanish negative informal commands 5. Italian subjunctive 6. French subjunctive	1. Benati 2004b 2. Farley 2001, 2004 3. Wong 2004 4. Lee & Benati with Aguilar-Sánchez & McNulty 2007 5. Lee & Benati 2007 6. Lee & Benati 2007
Principle 1f. The Sentence Location Principle. Learners tend to process items in sentence initial position before those in final position and those in medial position.	1. Spanish copula 2. Spanish preterite tense 3. Italian future tense 4. Spanish subjunctive 5. English simple past tense 6. Japanese affirmative and negative present tense 7. Spanish preterite/ imperfect distinction	1. Cheng 2002, 2004 2. Cadierno 1995 3. Benati 2001, 2004a 4. Farley 2001, 2004 5. Benati 2005 6. Lee & Benati 2007 7. Lee & Benati with Aguilar-Sánchez & McNulty 2007

The Immediate Effects of PI Compared to Those of TI and MOI

The effects of PI on grammatical development have been empirically compared to two other types of grammar instruction, traditional instruction (TI) and meaning-based output instruction (MOI). The differences between the two types of instruction are delineated more fully in Chapter 2. Both types have learners practicing grammar though output practices.

The research we presented in this volume adds in important ways to the body of work on the immediate effects of PI compared to those of TI. As Lee (2004; p. 321) pointed out, a review of research on PI clearly attests to its generalisability to learners whose native language is English as they learn a Romance language. Benati (Benati 2005; Lee and Benati 2006) has added a tremendously important element to PI research through his investigations of non-Romance languages. By investigating English and Japanese as second languages with learners whose native languages are Greek, Chinese, and Italian, he has greatly added to the generalisability of PI findings. His findings with non-Romance languages mirrors those with Romance Languages; his findings with native speakers of languages other than English mirror those with native speakers of English. His work lends positive support to two of Lee's hypotheses (Lee 2004; p. 321–322).

> Hypothesis 3. PI can help learners of any L2 to process a formal feature of that language in order to determine an appropriate semantic interpretation of a sentence.

> Hypothesis 7. PI will be effective for instilling target-language specific processing strategies, no matter the L1 of the learners.

We have updated Table 2.2 from Chapter 2 to now include the research we presented in this volume. Table 6.2 presents a summary of the effects of PI compared to TI on interpretation and production tasks.

Table 6.2   Revised Summary of The Immediate Effects of PI Compared to Those of TI

Study	Linguistic Item	Interpretation Results	Production Results
VanPatten & Cadierno 1993	Spanish object pronouns	PI > (TI = C)	(PI = TI) > C
Cadierno 1995	Spanish preterite tense	PI > (TI = C)	(PI = TI) > C

Study	Linguistic Item	Interpretation Results	Production Results
Benati 2001	Italian future tense	PI > TI > C	(PI = TI) > C
Cheng 2002	Spanish copula	PI > (TI = C)	(PI = TI) > C
VanPatten & Wong 2004	French causative	PI > TI > C	(PI = TI) > C
Cheng 2004	Spanish copula	—	(PI = TI) > C
Benati 2005	English simple past	PI > TI = MOI	PI = TI = MOI
Lee & Benati 2007	Japanese past tense	PI > TI	PI = TI
Lee & Benati 2007	Japanese affirmative vs. negative present tense	PI > TI	PI = TI

PI = Processing Instruction
TI = Traditional Instruction
C = Control group
MOI = Meaning-based Output Instruction

The research we presented in this volume adds much to the discussion of the relative effects of PI and MOI. Farley (2001b, 2004) has asserted that PI is not more effective than MOI when the grammar item is complex, as is the Spanish subjunctive of doubt. Benati's research in this volume definitively lays that argument to rest. When comparing the effects of PI and MOI on Italian and French subjunctives of doubt, which are as equally complex as the Spanish subjunctive of doubt, he finds that the effects of PI are superior to those of MOI on interpretation tasks and equal to each other on production tasks. Benati's findings are all the stronger in that he has them for instruction delivered in two different modes, classroom and computer. Add the findings from Benati (2005) in which the effects of MOI were equal to the effects of TI and we are left to wonder what methodological fluke produced Farley's findings.

We have updated Table 2.4 from Chapter 2 to now include the research we presented in this volume. Table 6.3 presents a summary of the effects of PI compared to MOI on interpretation and production tasks.

Table 6.3   Revised Summary of The Immediate Effects of PI Compared to Those of MOI

Study	Linguistic Item	Interpretation	Production
Farley 2001a	Spanish subjunctive N =29	PI > MOI	PI = MOI
Farley 2001b, a2004	Spanish subjunctive N= 50	PI = MOI	PI = MOI
Benati 2005	English simple past Greek L1	PI > MOI = TI	PI = MOI =TI
	Chinese L1	PI > MOI = TI	PI = MOI =TI
Lee & Benati 2007	Italian subjunctive	PI > MOI classroom PI > MOI computer	PI = MOI classroom PI = MOI computer
Lee & Benati 2007	French subjunctive	PI > MOI classroom PI > MOI computer	PI = MOI classroom PI = MOI computer

PI = Processing Instruction
TI = Traditional Instruction
MOI = Meaning-based Output Instruction

Modes of Delivering PI: Classroom and Computers

The research we have presented in this volume adds a completely new dimension to what we know about the effects of PI on promoting second language grammatical development. As the summary of our results in Table 6.4 shows, PI is equally effective in promoting second language development no matter the mode of delivering the instruction. Classroom and computer delivery of PI yielded identical results across three languages (Spanish, Italian, French) and three linguistic items/structures (preterit/imperfect distinction, negative informal commands, subjunctive of doubt).

Table 6.4   Summary of the Effects of Modes of Delivering PI (this volume)

Author	Linguistic item	Modes	Results
Lee & Benati with Aguilar-Sánchez & McNulty	Preterit/imperfect distinction	Classroom, computer, hybrid	Assessment: multiple choice item selection
			Classroom = computer = hybrid on both post-tests
Lee & Benati with Aguilar-Sánchez & McNulty	Negative informal commands	Classroom, computer, hybrid	Assessment: multiple choice item selection
			Classroom = computer = hybrid on both post-tests
Lee & Benati	Italian subjunctive	Classroom, computer	Assessment: Interpretation task
			Classroom = computer
			Assessment: Production task
			Classroom = computer
Lee & Benati	French subjunctive	Classroom, computer	Assessment: Interpretation task
			Classroom = computer
			Assessment: Production task
			Classroom = computer

Conclusions

We have long worked with PI in both our classroom teaching and our research. We have seen its tenets supported with a host of empirical works. We are firmly convinced that PI is good and effective instruction. As we stated in Chapter 2, previous PI research has focused on two issues: the effects of PI compared to other types of instruction and the roles of structured input and explicit information in the effects of PI. In this volume we have contributed more information to the first of these issues. Additionally, we have forged a new line of PI investigation: whether the effects of PI are sensitive to the modes in which PI is delivered. Based on our findings we offer the following conclusions.

1. PI is an effective intervention for addressing a variety of L2 processing problems, in Romance and non-Romance languages, and with native speakers of a variety of L1s.

2. PI is more effective than other types of instruction (TI or MOI) when learners' performance is assessed with interpretation tasks.

3. PI is as equally effective as other types of instruction (TI or MOI) when learners are assessed with form-focused production tasks.

4. PI is an effective intervention no matter the mode (computer or classroom) in which it is delivered to L2 learners.

Recommendations for the Practice of PI

One of the main concerns of input processing is how learners perceive and process linguistic data in the language they hear or read. The question is: how do learners get linguistic data from the input? Research on input processing has attempted to describe what linguistic data learners attend to and what they do not attend to. From this research, VanPatten has introduced a number of psycholinguistic principles that L2 learners rely on when processing input (VanPatten 1996, 2004b). As we argued in Chapter 1 the role of L2 instruction is to help form and direct whatever internal processes learners bring to the task of language learning.

One of the questions addressed by scholars who have carried out research on the effects of instruction from a processing perspective is: can input processing be manipulated, altered or enhanced in order to make intake grammatically richer? This question has directly led to the development of PI, whose main aim is 'to push to get L2 learners to make form-meaning mappings in order to create grammatically richer intake' (VanPatten 1996:55). PI was developed with the aim of pushing L2 learners to attend to elements in the input that might otherwise be missed. The main purpose of PI is not to 'pour knowledge' into learners' heads, but to assist certain cognitive processes which can aid the growth of the developing system by enriching learners' intake. PI accomplishes its goal of manipulating learners' processing strategies; the result being that learner's develop the ability to interpret and produce sentences using a targeted linguistic feature. Research reviewed in Chapter 2 has highlighted that the main factor responsible for the positive results in learners' performance in PI studies is the input practice. Structured input activities are responsible for pushing learners to process forms in the input that might otherwise go unnoticed. The new data presented in Chapter 3 support the previous research that structured input is the causative variable for the improved performance of learners of Japanese.

Based on the new empirical evidence we provided in Chapters 4 and 5 that investigated the effects of delivering PI in different modes, plus the overall findings of PI research conducted to date, we can draw some pedagogical implications. First, our findings when placed in the larger research context (see Tables 6.1–6.3) affirm that PI is an effective instructional intervention that allows for a focus on form within a communicative framework. We promote PI as an educational benefit in that with PI learners get two-for-one. That is, learners only practice interpreting sentences, but they get the double benefit of being able to interpret sentences and produce correct forms. Second, from the two empirical studies reviewed in this book which that different modes of delivering PI (computer delivery, instructor delivery, and paper delivery) we have concluded that PI is beneficial instruction no matter the mode of delivery nor the grammatical feature. PI is undoubtedly an effective way to incorporate a focus on form into a communicative framework. Using the computer to deliver PI is also effective. For those who wish to make instruction more efficient, we recommend that they look to the computer to offer some parts of instruction. We hasten to add that our findings across three languages and three grammatical items show that the computer is not better at delivering PI than a classroom instructor. But, the computer offers other advantages such as allowing learners access to instructional materials in accordance with their own schedules. For those who wish to develop their own materials, we have offered many examples of structured input activities throughout this book. We also recommend Chapter 7 of Lee and VanPatten (2003) in which they provide guidelines for developing structured input activities as well as examples of different types of structured input activities. We also recommend Farley (2005) in which he demonstrates structured input activities for three of VanPatten's processing principles. Readers new to structured input or new to creating structured input activities will benefit from reading Chapter 5 of Farley in which he describes common pitfalls and addresses frequently asked questions for those who set out to design structured input activities. Structured input activities have also been incorporated into several textbooks including online materials (Lee, Young, McGuire, and Binkowski, 2005; VanPatten, Glass, Binkowski, Lee and Ballman 2006).

Our final pedagogical implication has to do with the role of output in second language acquisition. The research results are conclusive that PI is superior to TI. The results are, however, mixed when PI is compared with MOI. Our research comparing PI and MOI find that PI is superior to MOI. Our final pedagogical recommendation is the develop materials that move learners from first processing input to then producing output. We refer the readers Figures 1.1, 1.2 and 1.3 for a schematic of second language acquisition that supports this recommendation. By processing input, learners make the form-meaning connections needed for intake. By producing output, learners develop accuracy and fluency as well as communicative language ability (Lee 2000a; Lee and VanPatten 2003). We recommend VanPatten 2003, in which he develops fully his positions on moving from input to output in instructed second language acquisition.

Lee (2000a: 11) has assigned a specific role for output as the role that 'output plays in language development is to push learners to develop communicative language ability'. Input practice pushes learners to connect a particular meaning with a particular form. Our concept for output practice as related to grammar instruction is parallel. Output practice, as part of grammar instruction, should push learners to express a particular meaning via a particular form. Specifically, we advocate the use of structured ouput practices (Lee and VanPatten 1995, 2003). As previously stated by Lee and VanPatten (1995: 121) structured output activities have two main characteristics: they involve the exchange of previously unknown information; and, they require learners to access a particular form or structure in order to express meaning.

Lee and VanPatten (2003: 154) offer the following guidelines for developing structured output activities:

1) present one thing a the time

2) keep meaning in focus

3) move from sentences to connected discourse

4) use both written and oral output

5) others must respond to the content of the output

Since we have provided many examples of structured input activities in this book, we now provide examples of structured output activities. Again, our recommendation is that learners first be provided structured input activities followed by structured output activities. We refer the reader to Morgan-Short and Bowden (2006) for an example of how to adapt structured output activities to computer-delivery.

In the example in Activity A the focus is on one form and one meaning (talking about past events) and learners must respond to the content of the output.

Activity A « Your instructor's holiday »

Step 1

You will hear the first part of a sentence about your instructor's holiday. Change the verb in brackets to complete the sentence.

1 _____ (visit) his parents
2 _____ (have) a good time
3 _____ (talk) to people
4 _____ (play) football
5 _____ (crash) his car

Sentence heard by learner:

1. *He went to Italy and he.....*
2. *When he was there he.....*
3. *When he was there he....*
4. *When he was there he....*
5. *However, at the end of the holiday he....*

Step 2 How did you spend your holiday?

Present your sentences to your partner. Your partner will also present his sentences to you (write them in the chart below).

Myself	My friend

Step 3

Compare the sentences to find out who had the most enjoyable holiday!

In Activity B we provide another example of structured output activities. In this case learners must complete the sentence using the subjunctive forms In Italian to express doubt and opinion.

Activity B « Il Principe Carlo »

You will hear the beginning of a sentence which you need to complete by putting the verb in brackets at the appropriate tense. Then decide if you agree or not with the sentences by ticking the right box.

		Sono d'accordo	Non sono d'accordo
1	_____ (dovere) risposarsi.	❑	❑
2	_____ (essere) un buon reale.	❑	❑
3	_____ (essere) un buon padre.	❑	❑
4	_____ (avere) molte qualità umane.	❑	❑
5	_____ (fare) buone cose.	❑	❑

Sentence heard by learner:

1. *Non credo che…*
2. *Dubito che…*
3. *Sono certo che…*

4. *Non penso che ...*
5. *Sono certo che...*

In Activity C learners must produce subjunctive forms in French based on the triggers they have heard. Learners heard the first part of the sentence and they were required to produce either indicative or subjunctive (infinitive of the verb was provided in brackets) based on the triggers heard.

Activity C « La reine Elizabeth »

You will hear the beginning of a sentence which you need to complete by putting the verb in brackets at the appropriate tense. Then decide if you agree or not with the sentences by ticking the right box.

		D'accord	Pas d'accord
1	_____ (faire) le ménage elle-même.	❏	❏
2	_____ (recevoir) Jacques Chirac bientôt.	❏	❏
3	_____ (construire) ses chapeaux.	❏	❏
4	_____ (suivre) l'actualité.	❏	❏
5	_____ (peindre).	❏	❏
6	_____ (vouloir) se remarier.	❏	❏

Sentence heard by learner:

1. *Je ne crois pas que la reine d'Angleterre...*
2. *Il est possible qu'elle...*
3. Je doute qu'elle...
4. Je pense qu'elle...
5. *Je ne pense pas qu'elle...*
6. *Je ne suis pas sûr qu'elle...*

In Activity D we provide an example of a MOI activity in Japanese. This activity as in the case of previous examples is a follow-up structured output activities that learners would be asked to complete after they have been practising the past tense through structured input activities. In this activity the focus is on one form and one meaning and learners are asked to talk about past events (in this case talk about how they spend their week-end). Learners were asked to use a particular form (past forms in Japanese) to express a particular meaning (how they spend their week-end) and are involved in exchanging previously unknown information and using that information to establish who had the best week-end.

Activity D « Your instructor's week-end »

Step 1

You will hear the first part of a sentence about your instructor's week-end. Change the verb in brackets (Japanese present forms) to complete the sentence.

   1. Shumatsu watashi wa tomodachi to _____ (sugoshimasu).
   2. Watashi wa terebi de totemo ii eiga o _____(mimasu).
   3. Watashi wa Paul to kouen o _____ (arukimasu).
   4. Watashi wa bar de wain o takusan _____ (nomimasu).
   5. Watashi wa totemo ii hon o _____(yomimasu).

Sentence heard by learner:

   1. *Shumatsu watashi wa tomodachi to sugoshimashita.*
   2. *Watashi wa terebi de totemo ii eiga o mimashita.*
   3. *Watashi wa Paul to kouen o arukimashita.*
   4. *Watashi wa bar de wain o takusan nomimashita.*
   5. *Watashi wa totemo ii hon o yomimashita.*

Step 2

What did you do at the week-end?

Present your sentences to your partner. Your partner will also present his sentences to you (write them in the chart below).

Myself	My Partner

Step 3

Compare the sentences to find out who had the most interesting week-end!

These four activities serve to demonstrate the progression from structured input to structured output. Once learners have connected a particular meaning with a particular form, they should then be pushed to express that particular meaning using that particular form.

References

Barcroft, J. and VanPatten, B. (1997) Acoustic salience of grammatical forms: The effect of location stress, and boundedness on Spanish L2 input processing. In W. R. Glass and A. Pérez-Leroux (eds) *Contemporary Perspectives on the Acquisition of Spanish: Production, Processing, and Comprehension* (109–121) Sommerville, MA: Cascadilla Press.

Bardovi-Harlig, K. (1992) The use of adverbials and natural order in the development of temporal expression. *International Review of Applied Linguistics* 30, 299–320.

Benati, A. (2001) A comparative study of the effects of processing instruction and output-based instruction on the acquisition of the Italian future tense. *Language Teaching Research* 5, 95–127.

Benati, A. (2004a) The effects of structured input and explicit information on the acquisition of Italian future tense. In B. VanPatten (ed.) *Processing Instruction: Theory, Research, and Commentary* (207–255) Mahwah, NJ: Erlbaum.

Benati, A. (2004b) The effects of processing instruction and its components on the acquisition of gender agreement in Italian. *Language Awareness* 13, 67–80.

Benati, A. (2005) The effects of PI, TI and MOI in the acquisition of English simple past tense. *Language Teaching Research* 9, 67–113.

Benati, A. and Romero Lopez, P. (2003) The effects of structured input and explicit information on the acquisition of gender agreement in Italian and the simple paste tense in Spanish. In G. White (eds) *Applied Linguistics at the Interface* (29–46) London: Equinox.

Benati, A., VanPatten, B. and Wong, W. (2005) *Input Processing and Processing Instruction*. Rome: Armando Editore.

Bransdorfer, R. (1989) Communicative value and linguistic knowledge in second language oral input processing. Unpublished doctoral thesis, University of Illinois, Champaign-Urbana.

Buck, M. (2000) Procesamiento del lenguaje y adquisición de una segunda lengua. Un estudio de la adquisición de un punto gramatical en inglés por hispanohablantes. Unpublished doctoral thesis, Universidad Nacional Autónoma de México, Mexico City.

Cadierno, T. (1995) Formal instruction from a processing perspective: An investigation into the Spanish past tense. *The Modern Language Journal* 79, 179–93.

Cadierno, T. and Glass, W. R. (1990) Competing forms in the input: An investigation of how learners process past tense. Paper presented at The Annual Meeting of The American Association of Teachers of Spanish and Portuguese Miami.

Chang, K-Y and Smith,W. F. (1991) Cooperative learning and CALL/IVD in beginning Spanish: An experiment. *Modern Language Journal* 75, 205–211.

Cheng, A. (1995) Grammar instruction and input processing: The acquisition of Spanish *ser* and *estar*. Unpublished doctoral thesis, the University of Illinois, Urbana-Champaign.

Cheng, A. (2002) The effects of processing instruction on the acquisition of ser and estar. *Hispania* 85, 308–323.

Cheng, A. (2004) Processing instruction and Spanish *ser* and *estar*: Forms with semantic-aspectual value. In B. VanPatten (ed.) *Processing Instruction: Theory, Research, and Commentary* (119–141) Mahwah, NJ: Erlbaum.

Doughty, C. and Williams, J. (eds) (1998) *Focus on Form in Classroom Second Language Acquisition.* Cambridge University Press.

Farley, A. P. (2001a) The effects of processing instruction and meaning-based output instruction. *Spanish Applied Linguistics* 5, 57–94.

Farley, A. P. (2001b) Authentic processing instruction and the Spanish subjunctive. *Hispania* 84, 289–299.

Farley, A. (2004a) The relative effects of processing instruction and meaning-based output instruction. In B. VanPatten (ed.) *Processing Instruction: Theory, Research, and Commentary* (143–168) Mahwah, NJ: Erlbaum.

Farley, A. (2004b) Processing instruction and the Spanish subjunctive: Is explicit information needed? In B. VanPatten (ed.) *Processing Instruction: Theory, Research, and Commentary* (227–239) Mahwah, NJ: Erlbaum.

Farley A. (2005) *Structured Input: Grammar Instruction for the Acquisition-Oriented Classroom.* New York: McGraw-Hill.

Gely, A. (2005) Output-Based Instruction versus Processing Instruction on the acquisition of the French imperfect tense. Unpublished Master's thesis, University of Greenwich, London.

Harrington, M. (2004) Commentary: Input processing as a theory of processing input. In B. VanPatten (ed.) *Processing Instruction: Theory, Research, and Commentary* (79–92) Mahwah, NJ: Erlbaum.

Hulstijn, J. (1989) Implicit and incidental language learning: Experiments in the processing of natural and partly artificial input. In H. Dechert and M. Raupach (eds) *Interlingual Processes* (49–73) Tubingen: Gunter Narr.

Klein, W. (1986) *Second Language Acquisition.* Cambridge University Press.

Krashen, S. (1982) *Principles and Practice in Second Language Acquisition.* London: Pergamon.

Lee, J. F. (1999) On levels of processing and levels of comprehension. In J. Gutiérrez-Rexach and F. Martínez-Gil (eds) *Advances in Hispanic Linguistics: Papers from the Second Hispanic Linguistics Symposium: Vol. 1* (42-59). Somerville, MA: Cascadilla.

Lee, J. (2000a) *Tasks and Communicating in Language Classrooms.* New York: McGraw-Hill.

Lee, J. (2000b) Five types of input and the various relationships between form and meaning. In J. F. Lee and A. Valdman (eds) *Form and Meaning: Multiple Perspectives* (25–42) Boston: Heinle and Heinle.

Lee, J. (2003) Cognitive and linguistic perspectives on the acquisition of object pronouns in Spanish. In B. Lafford and R. Salaberry (eds) *Spanish Second Language Acquisition: State of the Science* (98–129) Washington, D.C.: Georgetown University Press.

Lee, J. (2004) On the generalizability, limits, and potential future directions of processing instruction research. In B. VanPatten (ed.) *Processing Instruction: Theory, Research, and Commentary* (311–323) Mahwah, NJ: Erlbaum.

Lee J, Cadierno T, VanPatten, B. and Glass, W. (1997) The effects of lexical and grammatical cues on processing past temporal reference in second language input. *Applied Language Learning* 8, 1–27.

Lee, J. and VanPatten, B. (1995) *Making Communicative Language Teaching Happen.* New York: McGraw-Hill.

Lee, J. and VanPatten, B. (2003) *Making Communicative Language Teaching Happen, 2nd ed.* New York: McGraw-Hill.

Lee, J. Young, D., McGuire, S. and Binkowski, D. (2005) *Online Manual to Accompany ¿Qué te parece? 3rd.* New York: McGraw-Hill.

Liu, M., Moore, Z., Graham, L. and Lee, S. (2002) A look at the research on computer-based technology use in second language learning: A review of the literature from 1990–2000. *Journal of Research on Technology in Education* 34, 250–273.

Long, M. (1983) Does second language instruction make a difference? *TESOL Quarterly* 17, 359–82.

Mangubhai, F. (1991) The processing behaviours of adult second language learners and their relationship to second language proficiency. *Applied Linguistics* 12, 268–297.

Morgan-Short, K. and Bowden, H. W. (2006) Processing instruction and meaningful output-based instruction: Effects on second language development. *Studies in Second Language Acquisition* 28, 31–65.

Musumeci, D. (1989) The ability of second language learners to assign tense at the sentence level: A cross-linguistic study. Unpublished doctoral thesis, the University of Illinois, Urbana-Champaign.

Paulston, C. (1972) Structural patterns drills: A classification. In H. Allen and R. Campbell (eds) *Teaching English as a Second Language* (129–138) New York: McGraw-Hill.

Romero-López, P. (2002) Structured input activities or explicit information as main causative variable on the acquisition of Spanish preterit. Unpublished Master's thesis, University of Greenwich, London.

Salaberry, R. (2000) The development of past tense morphology in L2 Spanish. Amsterdam/Philadelphia: John Benjamins.

Sanz, C. (1997) Experimental tasks in SLA research: Amount of production, modality, memory and production processes. In W. R. Glass and A. T. Perez-Leroux (eds) *Contemporary Perspectives on the Acquisition of Spanish:*

Production, Processing, and Comprehension (41–56) Sommerville, MA: Cascadilla Press.

Sanz, C. (2004) Computer delivered implicit versus explicit feedback in processing instruction. In B. VanPatten (ed.) *Processing Instruction: Theory, Research, and Commentary* (241–255) Mahwah, NJ: Erlbaum.

Sciarone, A. and Meijer, P. (1993) How free should students be? A case from CALL: Computer-assisted language learning. *Computers Educ.* 21, 95–101.

Sharwood-Smith, M. (1986) Comprehension versus acquisition: Two ways of processing input. *Applied Linguistics* 7, 239–274.

Sharwood-Smith, M. (1993) Input enhancement in instructed SLA: Theoretical bases. *Studies in Second Language Acquisition* 15, 165–179.

Skehan, P. (1989) *Individual Differences in Second-Language Learning*: Edward Arnold.

Spada, N. (1997) Form-focused instruction and second language acquisition: A review of classroom and laboratory research. *Language Teaching* 30, 73–87.

Stevick, E. (1976) *Memory, Meaning, and Method*. Rawley, MA: Newbury House.

Terrell, T. D. (1986) Acquisition in the Natural Approach: The Binding\Access Framework. *The Modern Language Journal* 70, 213–228.

Terrell T. D. (1991) The role of grammar instruction in a communicative approach. *The Modern Language Journal* 75, 52–63.

VanPatten, B. (1985) Communicative value and information processing in second language acquisition. In E. Judd, P. Nelson and D. Messerschmitt (eds) *On TESOL '84: A Brave New World* (88–99) Washington, D.C.: TESOL.

VanPatten, B. (1990) Attending to content and form in the input: An experiment in consciousness. *Studies in Second Language Acquisition* 12, 287–301.

VanPatten, B. (1993) Grammar instruction for the acquisition rich classroom. *Foreign Language Annals 26,* 433–450.

VanPatten, B. (1996) *Input Processing and Grammar Instruction: Theory and Research.* Norwood, NJ: Ablex.

VanPatten, B. (2000) Processing instruction as form-meaning connections: Issues in theory and research. In J. F. Lee and A. Valdman (eds) *Form and Meaning: Multiple Perspectives* (43–68) Boston: Heinle and Heinle.

VanPatten, B. (2002) Processing instruction: An update. *Language Learning 52,* 755–803.

VanPatten, B. (2003) *From Input to Output: A Teacher's Guide to Second Language Acquisition.* New York: McGraw-Hill.

VanPatten, B. (ed) (2004a) *Processing Instruction: Theory, Research, and Commentary.* Mahwah, NJ: Erlbaum.

VanPatten, B. (2004b) Input processing in second language acquisition. In B. VanPatten (ed.) *Processing Instruction: Theory, Research, and Commentary* (5–31) Mahwah, NJ: Erlbaum.

VanPatten, B. (2004c) Several reflections on why there is good reason to continue researching the effects of processing instruction. In B. VanPatten (ed.) *Processing Instruction: Theory, Research, and Commentary* (325–335) Mahwah, NJ: Erlbaum.

VanPatten, B. and Cadierno, T. (1993) Explicit instruction and input processing. *Studies in Second Language Acquisition 15,* 225–243.

VanPatten, B., Glass, W., Binkowski, D., Lee, J. and Ballman, T. (2006) *Online Workbook to Accompany Vistazos 2nd.* New York: McGraw-Hill.

VanPatten, B. and Fernández, C. (2004) The long-term effects of processing instruction. In B. VanPatten (ed.) *Processing Instruction: Theory, Research, and Commentary* (273–289) Mahwah, NJ: Erlbaum.

VanPatten, B., Lee, J. F. and Ballman, T. (2006) *Viztazos: Un curso breve.* New York: McGraw-Hill.

VanPatten, B. and Oikennon, S. (1996) Explanation vs. structured input in processing instruction. *Studies in Second Language Acquisition 18,* 495–510.

VanPatten, B. and Sanz, C. (1995) From input to output: Processing instruction and communicative tasks. In F. R. Eckman, D. Highland, P. W. Lee, J. Mileham and R. R. Weber (eds) *Second Language Acquisition Theory and Pedagogy* (169–185) Mahwah, NJ: Erlbaum.

VanPatten, B. and Wong, W. (2004) Processing instruction and the French causative: Another replication. In B. VanPatten (ed.) *Processing Instruction: Theory, Research, and Commentary* (97–118) Mahwah, NJ: Erlbaum.

Wong, W. (2004a) The nature of processing instruction. In B. VanPatten (ed.) *Processing Instruction: Theory, Research, and Commentary* (33–63) Mahwah, NJ: Erlbaum.

Wong. W. (2004b) Processing instruction in French: The roles of explicit information and structured input. In B. VanPatten (ed.) *Processing Instruction: Theory, Research, and Commentary* (187–205) Mahwah, NJ: Erlbaum.

Wong, W. (2005) *Input Enhancement: From Theory and Research to the Classroom.* New York: McGraw-Hill.

Wong, W. and VanPatten, B. (2003) Then evidence is IN: Drills are OUT. *Foreign Language Annals 36,* 403–423.

Author index

Subject index

Printed in the United Kingdom
by Lightning Source UK Ltd.
131974UK00001BA/1/A

9 781845 532482